BRITISH SKYDIVING IN THE 1950s

Copyright © Bernard. A. N. Green 2020

ISBN 978-1-913218-84-3

Printed in Great Britain by
Biddles Books Limited, King's Lynn, Norfolk

CONTENTS

PREFACE 1
FREE-FALL 2
FREE-FALL FROM 1,500Ft 9
JIM BASNETT JULY 1959 10
THE BIG BRA 11
BIG BUM 12
THE TIGER MOTH 13
THE OAK TREE 15
GQ SHAPED 20 ft No 352206 18
SANDOWN ISLE OF WIGHT 19
GQ 20ft at SANDOWN AIRPORT 23
MALFUNCTIONS 24
ALWAYS PACK YOUR OWN CHUTE 25
AMERICAN PARACHUTES 26
SOUTHDOWN SKYDIVERS 27
9TU-JUST FOR YOU. 31
CUTTING UP CHUTES 34
FED UP, FRED GAYLER 35
PARACHUTE SLEEVES 36
PARACHUTING PIONEERS 37
THE FRENCH EAGLE 38
CHALON-SUR-SOANE 38
INSTRUCTORS LICENCE 44
KIDLINGTON AIRPORT 45
JUMP INTO A RUBBISH DUMP 46

BIGGIN HILL	48
KIDLINGTON (OXFORD)	48
THE PICNIC	49
SLEEVES	50
WHERE'S THE BODY?	51
SKYDIVING EQUIPMENT 1960'S	56
THE AUSTER INCIDENT	59
SKYDIVING IN STYLE.	61
SKYDIVING, THE BLACK HOLE	67
FAI LICENCE	69
GREEN FLYER	69
THE PERSISTANT ASSISTANT	71
BRITISH PARACHUTE ASSOCIATION	74
'WILMSLOW'	78
THE DARK SIDE	79
FALLING OUT OVER SHOES	80
R.A.F WETHERSFIELD	84
BLACKBUSH	85
STAPLEFORD TAWNEY	86
BRITISH SKYDIVING LTD. THRUXTON	86
THE B17 FLYING FORTRESS	88
FOR THE TOSS OF A COIN	90
UNDER THE WIRES	92
THE INDIAN ROPE TRICK	94
PARACHUTING (THE SUIT)	101
A CHILL IN THE AIR	105
GINGER GREEN	108

COMPANY AMBULANCE	111
THE ENIGMATIC SMILE	111
CAMERA'S CAUSE CASUALTIES	116
DISPLAY TEAM	118
YOU MUST BE JOKING	119
THE JACKAROO	121
BRITISH SKYDIVING LTD	122
DE-HAVILLAND RAPIDE	122
THRUXTON, NIGHT JUMP	123
THRUXTON, LONGLEAT LIONS	125
HAIRY SCARY FOR BABY BERNIE	128
OVERLOADED	129
PLYMOUTH AIR RALLY	131
THE SHUTTLECOCK	134
THRUXTON, THE WILD SIDE	143
BPA MEMBERSHIP	146
THE BROWN BOMBER	147
ALLO-ALLO	148
MILITARY MEN	153
COLONEL R.D. WILSON	154
1st JUNE 1964.	154
SPORT PARACHUTIST. MAGAZINE	154
Lt RUDGE PENLEY	154
THE DE-HAVILLAND RAPIDE	155
BRITISH SKYDIVING CLUB	156
I BLEW IT APART	156
THE THRUXTON NEWSLETTER.	159

A BROKEN BACK	161
MY LAST SKYDIVE	164
BOB ACRAMEN	167
POEM FOR BOB	170
HALFPENNY GREEN CLOSED	171
CLOSURE OF BRITISH SKYDIVING LTD	171
BOB ACRAMEN, THE BUYER	176
TIM BETTIN, THE SKYDIVER	177
BPA 1960 TIMELINE	179
SPORT PARACHUTIST MAGAZINE	184
BPA INSTRUCTORS CONVENTION	184
ADRENALINE AND SANITY	186
FEAR	192

PREFACE

This book is a re-write of articles taken from two of my books. My first book DUNCE OR DYSLEXIC by Simpleton was an autobiography with a message to parents of dyslexic children. In that book there were many unhappy stories, so I interspersed those stories with my poetry.

My second book has the title PARACHUTES POEMS & POLEMICS. It continued with my autobiography but had many poems which are only suitable for adults. That has made me put together this book which is purely about the history of British parachuting which developed into the sport of Skydiving in the 1950-1960s.

I tried to keep the stories in chronological order but it did not always look correct.
I have also used the Bookman old style font Size14 to assist those with problems with reading and dyslexia like me.

Some of the photos are not high quality but they were taken on cameras which did not have the high standards of what is available today.
Most of my photography went missing after
I loaned them to an exhibition

THE SPARK

In 1944 aged ten years I watched the soldiers jumping from a tethered Barrage Balloon onto Queens Avenue in Aldershot, Hampshire.
At home I borrowed a square linen tablecloth, tied string to the four corners and climbed up on the kitchen roof, this was about 9ft high. Then I jumped and landed heavily onto the rose garden, luckily it had been dug over. But from that day I wanted to experience parachuting.

Most of my dreams as a child involved floating and flying just above the ground instead of walking.
I jumped again off the garage roof but banged and cut my head, perhaps that is why I was considered a simpleton by some people when I was young, but I am dyslexic and suffer from dyscalculia.

FREE-FALL

PARACHUTING IN THE 1950's
I had joined the Royal Engineers on the 8th of March 1954 and intended to transfer to the Parachute Regiment but a friend of mine who was a Physical Training Instructor told me not to do it as it was too arduous and you only got eight jumps in a year.

So, I joined the parachute club at Fairoaks-Aerodrome Nr Woking in Surrey. This club was sponsored by the GQ Parachute Company of Woking I did my first eight jumps there. My first jump was on the 9th July1958, these were not static line jumps but free-fall, counting three seconds then pulling the ripcord. And that was from 1,500ft. It did not feel very high as you could recognize people's faces watching you from the ground.

There was a club room and a shed where the parachutes were packed. They had about six GQ parachutes supplied by GQ. They did not own an aircraft and hired an Auster four-seater aircraft or sometimes a Tiger Moth for those people that could jump without an instructor in attendance.

Jim Basnett was the Chief Instructor and he worked for the GQ Parachute Company at Woking. He also often flew the aircraft when dropping parachutists.

When I started Skydiving. I was still in the army as Postmaster at the Royal Engineers, Southwood Camp, Cove Nr Farnborough. Hants. Shown in the photo below. The Post office is the open door behind me. I was delivering the mail on my 650cc Triumph Bonneville motorbike while my associate postmen were still using their issue bicycles with no gears!

I got into a little trouble with the brigadier for wearing a Canadian olive-green gaberdine uniform. He asked where had I acquired it and why I was wearing it? I replied that I had bought it as it was smarter than the British uniform. Instead of putting me on a charge, he let me off after I promised not to wear it again and I appeared before him in my Royal Engineers uniform. I was very lucky that he had a sense of humour.

You can see in the photo below, that I was wearing shoes, I was not excused boots, I went into Aldershot and purchased military shoes, then excused my-self.

There is a very interesting story about my days as the Regimental policeman at this camp when I was in charge of the regiments prison.

The chapter is called The Hanging. That story is in Dunce or Dyslexic by Simpleton.

I was told that I was going to be sent to Egypt to fight at The Suez Conflict! But I wrote to the commanding officer and said, I would not fight a war because the 99year lease on the canal had expired. I was not sent to prison as I had expected but given The job in the post office instead.

CPL B. A. N. GREEN. RE.
JULY 1958

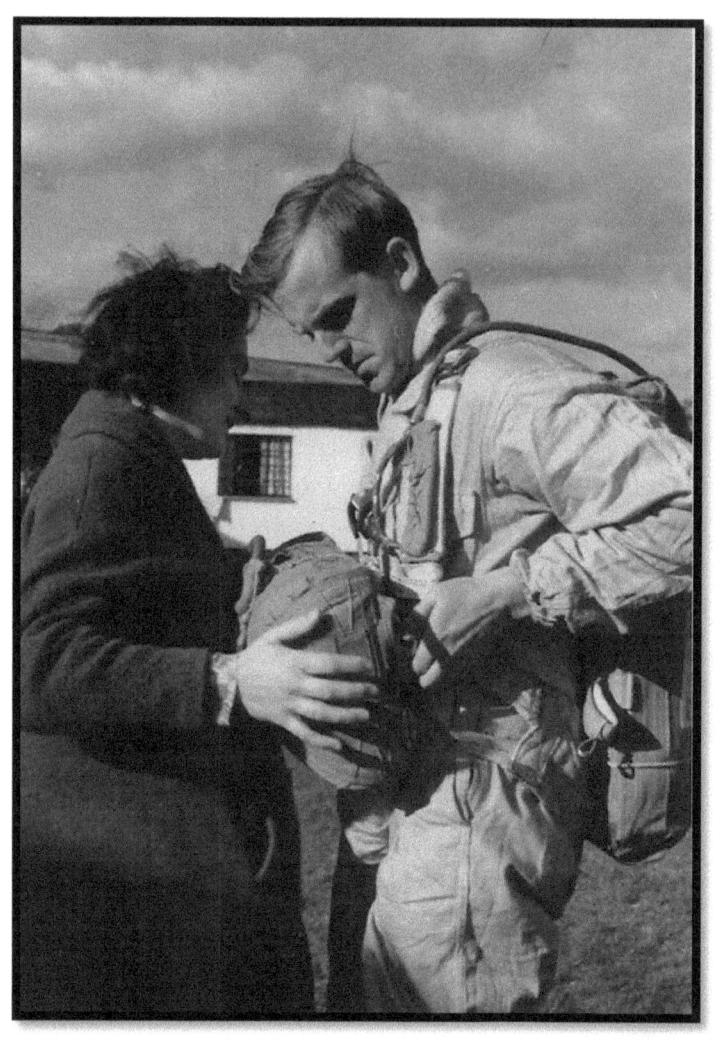

MY 1ˢᵗ FREE-FALL
9ᵗʰ JULY 1958

My wife Ann is helping to fit the G.Q. reserve chute. The main chute was a GQ 28ft.
She was pregnant with my son A. B. Green.

The aircraft was an Auster G-AIGU,
the pilot was Ron Cobbett
It was the 9th July 1958 when I did my first jump,
I wrote the following in my Logbook.

*First jump was done in an apprehensive mood knowing that I must do it to experience it. And very frightened but Peter Lang installs great confidence. On the way up Peter talked to give confidence.
I thought 1,500ft was not high enough but they must know what they are doing.
Feet out (The door) very scared "GO"
A blank space in my mind, I open my eyes-There is an aeroplane above my feet. Ye Gods I've left it-I'm falling-I've not counted, I Pull the ripcord-look up and see it streaming out (The Canopy)-Then a wonderful feeling-a lovely secure feeling. Look around, it's quiet up here- Grounds coming up fast, I'm there.*

I completed 35 jumps at Fairoaks Aerodrome before I left the club altogether.

13th October 1960 I received my parachuting certificate No. 57 signed by Lord Brabazon.

9th JULY 1958

I am waiting to board the aircraft for my first jump. Pauline Ady is in the centre of the photo. John Hogg has his arms folded and my wife Ann is second from the right.

The Aircraft was an Auster G-AIGU and the pilot was Ron Cobbett. Despatcher was Peter Lang.

FREE-FALL FROM 1,500Ft

JULY 1959

This was a chap called Ken O'Rourke free-falling from 1,500ft over Fairoaks Aerodrome in July 1958. The x on the concrete in front of the hanger is where I broke my coccyx. I have written about that in the story of the 'Big Brassiere'. Fairoaks is not a very big aerodrome and It was not uncommon for parachutists to land outside the airfield.

JIM BASNETT JULY 1959

Jim was the chief instructor of the British Parachute Club at Fairoaks aerodrome, which is near Woking in Surrey, UK.

He was employed by the GQ Parachute Company at Woking. He also flew the aircraft when used for parachuting.

He always wore his leathers when parachuting!

THE BIG BRA

21st JUNE 1959

When I started Parachuting, I was told that a malfunction only occurred in one of 20,000 descents. On the subject of reserve chutes, the practice was to open the reserve that was in front of you and grab a hand-full of canopy and throw it out to the side and try and get it away from the failed canopy above you. If you did not succeed, it would turn into a Roman-Candle and you would die. It got its name from when the reserve canopy rose into the main canopy and they both remain closed. As they were white and elongated it looked like a long white candle.

It was the 21st June 1959 when my 28ft round club parachute tried to turn inside out and ended up with three lines over the top of the canopy and it ended up looking like a big brassiere. It was spinning and when I threw the reserve it started to go up into what I said looked like a Big Bra, so I pulled it back and it wrapped around me like an Egyptian mummy. I could not see a thing. I got a smashed Coccyx when I landed on the concrete hangar apron.

I spent three days in hospital. It meant I could not sit down for a year, but I carried on jumping with a big rubber cushion sown into my jump-suit. It made me look as though I had a large posterior. The pain was terrible, I had crushed my Coccyx. If you do not know what that is, it is the remnant of our tail at the bottom of the spine. I could not sit on my bum, for about two years, I sat on my thigh. At the cinema I had to sit perched on the seat in the up position, much to the annoyance of anyone seated behind me. It is 60yrs now since that incident and every morning when I get up my bottom aches until I get moving.

It crushed the remains of my tail, the tail we had when we swung from tree to tree. Perhaps that is why we like jumping and falling free. I have had a pain in the bum for life, which made me a pain in the bum for my wife.

BIG BUM

I started parachuting again ten days later, on the 31st of July and won a competition at Fairoaks, if you see any photos of me it looks like I have a big bum, but I had a rubber cushion sewn into my orange coloured overalls. Orange? Yes. Was I not rather daring when everyone else had grey or white jump suits, and I also painted my helmet to make it look like the five-spotted ladybird! I had also purchased a brand-new type of GQ reserve parachute that when you pulled the handle it came out like a handbag, which you could then throw out away from the failed chute. So now I had a handbag as well as an orange jumpsuit and a Lady-bird helmet. Don't get ideas about me.

In two separate parachuting incidents I fractured my coccyx and my spine in three places, yet I am still able to touch my toes, so I am extremely lucky. The unusual reason is that I never had any plaster cast or treatment apart from physiotherapy which meant I kept my muscles. The specialist had told me "If I put you in plaster you will lose your muscles and it is your muscles that keep you standing, not your bones".

THE TIGER MOTH

When jumping from the Tiger Moth, as there were two separate cockpits the pilot sat in the back seat and the parachutist sat with one leg in the front cockpit and one leg outside and crouched forward to avoid the slipstream.

It was exciting and better still when at the required height and with a wave of your hand you asked the pilot to cut the throttle back; then you climbed out, closed the side hatch and secured it with a bolt. Then walked forward and while hanging onto the wing wires peered over the front of the lower wing with the heat of the exhaust beating on your face with the blast of the propeller. The forward speed at that time would be about 45mph.

Having ascertained or thought that you were in the correct position to fall and float to the landing site, you jumped off. *In those days there was no knowledge of Skydiving, you just fell.* After hooks on my hiking boots got hooked up for a while in the rigging of my deploying parachute canopy, I took up the habit of holding onto my toes in a Jack-knife diving position. This was before parachute sleeves came into use, prior to this the rigging was deployed from the backpack. The parachute cords were so tightly pulled into webbing loops that as they deployed it made you rock side to side as they pulled out.

On more than one occasion while I was at Fairoaks I saw that they did not come out of the webbing loops and the main parachute failed to open. Reserves were then thrown so we started attaching elastic bands to the webbing loops and the rigging was attached through them, any problem the elastic broke off.

Parachutes at that time were all circular white without any steering. All you could do is pull hard down on the harness risers to sideslip, but it did not make a lot of difference to where you were heading.

I only got ten jumps in my first year despite turning up every weekend. The reason being that too much time was spent with pencil and paper working out wind speed versus aircraft speed and ascertaining wind direction and waiting to hire aircraft.

Later when I attended the French Skydiving School at Chalon-Sur-Soane I learnt a valuable lesson. They owned their own aircraft and they just chucked a toilet roll out of the plane and watched where it landed to find the direction and distance. Their parachutes were far better than the British ones. The EFA 650 harness was comfortable and the chutes were steerable.

THE OAK TREE

11th JANUARY 1959

It was on my 11th jump on the 11th Jan 1959 that I floated over the Fairoaks aircraft hangers and landed in an oak tree beside the main road.
I crashed down through the branches but was not injured at all. Because my posterior was impaled on a barbed wire fence I decided to sit very still until rescued.

A lady drove past then reversed back to look at me. I just stared back at her; I was keeping very still. Because you do if you have wire barbs sticking in your bottom. Then the woman revved her engine very hard; then screamed off up the road. Funny woman I thought, why do that? Later we found out that she drove to the police station and reported a dead parachutist in a tree.

Oh, it is a good idea to keep your legs together when going down through tree branches.

On the 15th May 1959 I purchased a completely new rig from the GQ parachute Company, Number 352206. It had a harness with a big circular release box, and backpack with an orange and white quartered 20ft circular canopy. The cost was about £300.0.0. From this date I always packed my own parachute.

This canopy was a new design for jet aircraft as it was designed to open slowly at high velocity. When it opened, it reminded me of the big curtains at the cinema slowly opening, it nearly caught me out once, I have written about that in the story 'Where's the body'.

The reserve chute was a completely new design being packed in something like a woman's handbag. When required to use it the parachutist pulled the handle which released the bag and threw it out to the side where it would deploy and was in no danger of tangling with the main chute. I confidently wore this reserve for the next six jumps with the peace of mind of being over-confident.

Then I decided to repack it and to demonstrate the superiority of my latest acquisition, I invited all the

club members to watch as I stood on the packing table to pull and throw my handbag.
Please bear in mind I was not used to throwing handbags. I pulled and pulled, and it would not come out its case, so I asked other males to try to pull it out.

Nobody could budge it! It just would not work and yet on examination there was nothing that appeared to be wrong. I got a refund on the reserve, but perhaps I would not have got that refund if my main chute had failed in those ten jumps, that's an awful thought. In those early days at Fairoaks as we were jumping from 1,500ft in unstable positions with three second delays, this meant the chutes did not open quickly and cleanly. And there were only 10 seconds left before hitting the ground if you could not get the reserve deployed in the next 5 seconds.

I started travelling to other airfields where there were no height restrictions. This led to many adventures starting out with the peace of mind of being unaware of the problems that could and did occur. I reverted to using the American 24ft surplus reserve with the rip-stop nylon canopy. I never had another emergency to use a reserve chute again. I put this down to the training I got in France, and being in a stable face to earth position when deploying the chute, also I started using cotton sleeves to encase the main parachute, which I started to manufacture on my return from France and created British Skydiving Ltd.

GQ SHAPED 20 ft No 352206
MODIFIED.

The first time I used the above chute was on my 18th jump on the 31st of May 1959 from an Auster at 1,500 ft. After watching this chute open very slowly but surely due to only free-falling for 3seconds. I realized that I needed at the very least 5seconds free-fall to open it nicely. As I said before this GQ Shaped

20ft canopy opened slowly and gracefully rather like watching the large curtains at the theatre being opened. I got really attached to this chute perhaps because it brought me down safely so many times.

I did another twenty jumps with my parachute at Fairoaks and pushed the limit in seconds to ensure it opened. I also used the club chutes until I found other aerodromes that did not have an altitude restriction. It did not have steering until I cut panels out with a razor blade.

I did not modify this chute until the 16th of October 1960 and used it on my 68th jump at Thruxton Aerodrome. I was pleased with the steering and achieved my first stand-up landing.

It nearly caught me out at Sywell Aerodrome, it was the closest I have been to being killed. The story is called 'Where's the body'.

SANDOWN ISLE OF WIGHT

JULY 1959

It was at the end of July and beginning of August that members of the British Parachute club, gathered at Sandown Airport to enjoy some camping and falling from greater heights.

This is Pauline Ady in the photo.

Sandown Airport was all grass.
I am walking behind them. I regret I cannot name the other club member.

In July of 1959 I joined the club at Sandown Airfield on the Isle of Wight. On the 31st I did my 25th jump, a 12second freefall from 3,300ft. I was able to stabilise without any problem.

SANDOWN. From 2nd Right, Fred Gayler, Pauline Ady John Hogg, B. Green, Jim Basnett, and George Bottomer is on the far left.

On the 23rd July 1960 I had a 20 second delay From a Tiger Moth G-ARAZ piloted by George Bottomer. This was from 5,000ft, I had not noticed much while in the plane as I was keeping my head down out of the slipstream. When I left the aircraft I could see the whole island laid out below me, it was wonderful but then I thought 'Oh I might miss the island and land in the sea'. After ten seconds I did a back loop which felt quite natural as I had done some trampolining in the army.

AUGUST 1959

This photo shows me leaving the Tiger Moth over Sandown Airport, Isle of Wight.
I had neglected to close the cockpit side-hatch lid. You can see I painted my helmet as a five-spot ladybird. The bulge on my bottom is a cushion to avoid hurting my coccyx again as it was only 40 days since I crushed it. The view was worth the travelling. I neglected to record this jump.

GQ 20ft at SANDOWN AIRPORT

GQ No 52206.

This parachute had a slow deployment as it was for jet aircraft. I had jumped it for the first time at Fairoaks on the 31st May 1959. from 1,500ft. Thinking about it now, I think that I should have never jumped from less than 2,000ft with this parachute. When I was a young man, I only wore black, blue or grey, so it was quite outrageous to be 'in the pink'.

MALFUNCTIONS

AUGUST 1959

I want to tell you about malfunctions so that you can compare with the current situation.
On the 16th August 1959 This was my 30th jump, a 3second delay freefall at Fairoaks.
George Bottomer had jumped before me and had a streamer (Roman Candle) as the canopy cords had hooked onto his hiking boots.

I jumped from 1,500ft with a three second delay, this meant I was not falling fast enough for the club chute to open efficiently. The chute opened but with three lines over the top. The canopy looked a mess and started twirling around so I threw the reserve.

Because my descent rate was slow the reserve canopy dropped below me then rose up around me. I gathered it in my arms like gathering the washing. The main cleared itself and it was a soft landing. Makes me wonder now why I continued jumping?

I had been informed at the Fairoaks club that a parachute only malfunctioned once in 20.000 openings, but I had two malfunctions during the first year of my time at the club. My friend Martin Griffiths had three malfunctions that I am aware of when he threw and inflated his reserve chute. The dates were 1/08/1959-11/09/1960 and 17/06/1961.

John Hogg had a torn canopy on the 13th of March 1959 at Fairoaks Aerodrome.

Jean Webb threw her reserve on the 1st August 1969.

George Bottomer had a Roman Candle on the 16th Aug 1959 at Fairoaks and landed on his reserve chute.

Peter Lang who was my original instructor had a complete failure of his main parachute on a night jump from 2,000ft at Thruxton on 16/10/1960. He landed safely on his reserve, Peter Lang also had an incident which I wrote about in the story 'Parachuting, the Suit'.

ALWAYS PACK YOUR OWN CHUTE

My friend Martin and I had started parachuting at Fairoaks Aerodrome near Woking. The club was sponsored by the GQ Parachute Company and the Chief Instructor/Pilot was Jim Basnett. There was a Height restriction of 3,000ft at Fairoaks. My first jump was on 9/7/1958, the aircraft was an Auster, it was a three second free-fall from 1,500ft and my despatcher was Peter Lang. I must admit it did not seem high enough as I could recognize faces of the people on the ground. After pulling the ripcord I watched the chute stream past by feet and felt my shoulders rocking side to side as the lines were wrenched out of the wide webbing loops in the GQ backpack. On subsequent jumps I held onto my toes in a pike-dive position to avoid getting my legs in the rigging that is until I learnt to skydive correctly. It was soon after this that a club parachute roman candled because the rigging got stuck in the webbing loops. Following this we attached elastic bands to each webbing loop because they did not fail to release the parachute cords, if they snagged, they broke.

AMERICAN PARACHUTES

My first parachute that I purchased from the GQ Parachute Company was red and white quartered, it did not have steering. I started purchasing American War surplus chutes at a fraction of the new prices. They had never been issued and the USA military authorities sold them after they had been in storage for ten years, kept in airtight steel drums.

They had to be modified; I found a way of attaching British military surplus "D" rings to the harness to attach the reserve parachute. Also I cut out panels at the back of the canopy, this gave the chute a forward motion as the air filled the canopy and then flowed out the holes, this also stabilised the chutes descent because an uncut canopy rocked side to side as the air spilled out.

Starting in small steps we cut out two panels, the first ones were used for students and were called

Double L's and graduated to five panels and then it seemed that seven panels cut out was the absolute maximum for a very experienced person to jump with. Roughly speaking a five-gore cut out was 12 sq. feet, and a seven was about 16 sq. ft. I favoured the seven gore with a narrower cut.

SOUTHDOWN SKYDIVERS

Starting in 1959 a small group of us would arrive every weekend at Shoreham Airport on the South coast of England.

It was Martin Griffiths and I that went to Shoreham initially and obtained permission to parachute there. By the spring of 1960 we had a number of new members and recruits. Some of the names became well known in the Skydiving world, Mike Reilly from London, Peter Lang from Orpington, Kent. Pauline Ady. Peter Denley of Earls Court, London. Mick Reeves 1st Bn Parachute Regt. Les Boddy and Fred Gayler.

SHOREHAM

I am on the left and Martin on the right.
It was an exciting place to fly or parachute, we called ourselves 'The Southdown Skydivers'.

Not only are the surrounding chalk hills very beautiful, there is an Abbey on the hillside. As you take off and gain height the view stretches down the coast to the Isle of Wight, Portsmouth and Southampton. There are always a myriad of cruise and cargo ships and passing though these waters, and many private yachts. Not only that there was a café at the airport. We were soon joined by experienced jumpers and students.

Les Boddy and my-self. Fred Gayler in centre.
Mike Reilly and Pauline Ady on the right.

ISSY RONDEL.

There is a small Port at Shoreham with a very dangerous fast tidal flow in and out the river which passes under a road bridge on the eastern side of the Airport.

I can never forget a pupil called Issy Rondel, he always had a smile on his face, I remember he lived in London and was in the East End Rag trade.
At first, I thought he dealt in rags, a forerunner of the recycling business. How wrong can a person be, he designed and made dresses and had a factory in the east end of London. Not very tall and of stocky build, he was at the stage of free-fall and despatching himself.

He was incredibly lucky in a number of ways, he missed the airfield and drifted to the river, it was in full flood, he actually landed on the iron bridge parapet which was about 12 inches wide, I was running towards him as he teetered side to side with his arms flailing like windmills. Luckily the wind was light and did not pull him off and the chute collapsed onto the road, had it drifted the river side, he would have definitely been drowned.

9TU-JUST FOR YOU.

This was going to be an exciting day for me. I had already used both of my chutes and was eager to jump again, for here we had the height, meaning there were no height restrictions due to airline traffic. The only drawback was the single engine planes started to labour over 6000ft and costs started to rise. I noticed a packed American parachute that lay on the ground. I asked one of our club members, "Whose chute is that?" "Mine he replied, you can use it if you want". How kind of him I thought, quickly, before he changed his mind, I donned the chute and rushed to the Auster Aircraft.

I left the plane at 6,000ft, I had made sure that I was on the West side away from the river, I enjoyed the free-fall. It is quite interesting to note that there is plenty of time to enjoy the view, I noticed that on the west side the ground is very wet, with bog grass growing.

As the chute did not have any system of retarding the opening shock, it was quite a hard opening; these very often left bruising all over the chest. *Note, years later I had to have a Mastectomy, that's correct, not a Vasectomy, the continued bruising gave me a cancer, luckily it was benign, but it felt as though Shylock had cut away his pound of flesh from my chest after the operation.*

I looked up to check the chute, oh my goodness; I thought (or something similar) the shock has torn it to shreds. Then I looked closely. No; it had been severely cut right across the back. Eleven panels in all.

As you land it was common practice to hold on to the front risers to the canopy. The front of the canopy was cupping in and under, due to so much air rushing out the back and driving the chute forward. I was still about 1,500ft up so I gently pulled the risers down about three inches, the chute collapsed and candled, meaning it looks like a long white candle, many early parachutists met their death this way.

As I went to throw my reserve chute, the main chute cracked open with such force my right boot fell off, I was near the ground now and decided to leave everything alone; I dare not touch the parachute risers, the front panels were curling inwards very dangerously and could cause another collapse of the chute. I landed heavily into the lovely soft bog. Never found my boot. I spoke to the owner of the parachute briefly, He said it was an experimental idea that he had, but he had never used it. It was nice of him to lend it to me don't you think. Soon after this I started British Skydiving Ltd at Thruxton airfield.

BRITISH SKY-DIVING LTD.

Directors: B. Green. M. West. A. E. Green.

Tel: Runfold 2209 & 2587

Toll House,
Runfold,
Farnham, Surrey.

P R I C E   L I S T
19th February, – 1st April, 1966.

Item

1) **PARABOOTS.** Black leather, calf length, pneumatic soles, sizes 6½ – 12, buy now while we have your size in stock, do not wait for the Summer Rush.. — £9. 5. 0.
Plus postage .. — 4. 0.

2) **FRENCH JUMP SUITS.** Fully tailored, lots of pockets, full length zips, elasticated waist, Colours, Black, Orange.. — £9. 18. 0.
Plus postage. .. — 2. 0.

3) **BACK – PACK ASSEMBLY.** As new, assemble yourself, consisting of olive green B4 pack, harness, C9 Red/White ripstop canopy, white sleeve, drogue, ripcord.. — £50. 0. 0.
Double 'L' modification extra.. — £3. 0. 0.
Only a limited number at this special price.

4) **RESERVES.** British side pull, never used, manufactured in June, 1965. — £30. 0. 0.
5) T7 reserve, never used, olive green container, side pull, 24ft. white canopy. — £27. 10. 0.
6) T7, used good condition, olive green container, side pull, white 24ft. canopy. — £25. 0. 0.
7) British, used good condition, top pull. from — £15. 0. 0.
  to — £18. 0. 0.

8) **CANOPIES.** Excellent Condition.
A. 24ft. white twill for reserves — £9. 0. 0.
B. 28ft. C9 Red/White alternate, with risers — £26. 0. 0.
C. 28ft. C9 All White, with risers. — £26. 0. 0.
D. 28ft. C9 Red/White quarters, with risers — £26. 0. 0.
E. 24ft. white, with risers. — £18. 0. 0.

9) **EX. CLUB ASSEMBLIES.** Good condition. B4 Back pack assemblies, C9/double 'L's, 'TU's, visit club for details. Sale of this equipment due to both clubs refitting for summer courses. From— £30. 0. 0.

10) **MISCELLANEOUS.** A few only at reduced prices.
A. B4 containers, excellent condition.. — £6. 0. 0.
B. T7 reserve containers, good condition — £4. 0. 0.
C. New Ripcords, 4 pin and 2 pin.. — £1. 10. 0.
D. New B4 Harnesses, with "D" rings. — £9. 0. 0.
E. Pilot chutes, British. — £1. 0. 0.
F. Pilot chutes, hard top American — £2. 0. 0.
G. American Bubble Goggles, clear, lt.blue, lt.amber lt. green.. — £1. 4. 0.
H. B4 back pack cushions — 10. 0.

1ST APRIL 1966.   PRICE LIST.

CUTTING UP CHUTES

It was on the 31st May 1959 that I had purchased my first parachute from the GQ Parachute Company. It was red and white quartered ripstop nylon and had been designed for fighter jets. There-fore it was designed to open slowly otherwise it would get blown to pieces.

Soon after, I started purchasing American War surplus chutes at a fraction of the new prices. They had never been issued and the USA military authorities sold them after they had been in storage for ten years. They were as new as they had been kept in airtight steel drums. They were T7 Back-backs and T7 Reserves. The best feature about them was they had Capewell's, this was a way of detaching the canopy if you fell into water or being dragged, the British chutes did not have this system.

They had to be modified; I found a way of attaching British surplus "D" rings to the harness to attach the reserve parachute. Also I cut out panels at the back of the canopy, this gave the chute a forward motion as the air filled the canopy and then flowed out the holes, this also stabilised the chutes descent because an uncut canopy rocked side to side as the air spilled out.

Starting in small steps we cut out two panels, the first ones were used for students and were called Double L's, and then graduated to five panels and then it seemed that seven panels cut out was the absolute maximum for a very experienced person to jump with. Roughly speaking a five-gore cut out was 12 sq. feet, and a seven was about 16 sq. ft. I favoured the seven-gore cut with a narrower cut, any more cut out and the front of the canopy cusps in and a pull on the front risers would cause it to collapse as it did to me at Shoreham.

FED UP, FRED GAYLER

FRED AT FAIROAKS.
1st AUGUST 1959

Fred Gayler is the man that designed the first BPA (British Parachute Association) Emblem which I thought was perfect. It is illustrated later in this book.

PARACHUTE SLEEVES

The sleeves were like a long sock, the same length as the canopy with a flap turned back to stop the canopy coming out of the sleeve until the lines were completely deployed. The parachute cords were packed with rubber bands from loops holding the lines over that flap, this slowed the opening. This ensured a smooth deployment and reduced the shock load when falling from high altitude and having reached terminal velocity. Prior to the use of these sleeves we used to get covered in bruises from the harness and this caused me to have a Mastectomy due to a benign tumour. That was where the harness buckle bruised my breast.

If you wore a net type vest it left a bruise pattern all over your chest like a tattoo.

PARACHUTING PIONEERS

I do think that I am still alive partly because I read a lot of books on the early parachutists.
I had collected many books on early pioneers, many of whom died. A lot of them had their chutes tangle or Roman candle. A few died through experimenting with wings. The idea was to slow their decent rate; they knew that they could not land on small wings. They wanted to reduce their rate of fall from 120 mph so they could enjoy more time looking at the view. The first guy that jumped off the Eiffel Tower with wings and no chute did not have much time to enjoy the scenery.

I completed 41 jumps at Fairoaks, 24 on my own parachute, I used to stretch the 3sec Free-fall limit to make sure my parachute opened cleanly.

On my 15th jump I suffered concussion, and on the 38th jump as I walked back to the clubhouse, I could see two Tiger Moths coming towards me and I was running around trying to get away from them, but there was only one. I had double vision.

THE FRENCH EAGLE

8th SEPT 1959

I soon found out that I preferred the feeling of falling than being under the parachute; it is like lying on a very soft mattress with an amazing view. After averaging only two jumps a month at Fairoaks, in July 1959 my friends and I had started roaming around the country, in order to experience jumping from different aircraft at interesting venues with different views.

CHALON-SUR-SOANE

On the 8th Sept 1962 I went to Chalon-sur-Soane in France. Here I joined the French Army on a temporary basis to study their advanced Skydiving techniques under the command of Monsieur Bernard. I had done 111 parachute jumps by this time. It had taken me four years and three months to achieve.

Amazingly; I did six jumps the first day from a height of 2,500metres which included breakfast, lunch and tea and packing my own chute each time.
My first jump was really nerve racking but after that it was just practice. Now I will tell you about that first jump in France.

I could not speak a word of French and the instructors could speak English, but most refused to do so. The maximum height I had jumped from in the UK was 6,000ft. They issued me with a French steerable chute which would be the first time I had seen one and an altimeter showing height in metres, I was used to height being measured in good old British ft

We were placed into teams of four with two instructors per team. The aeroplane was a De-Havilland Rapide, registration F-BHCF. It had two engines and was built in the 1930's of wood and wire with a covering of cotton cloth. That sounds terrible, doesn't it? But I can tell you it was and is a wonderful safe plane.

I ended up owning a De-Havilland Rapide, number G-AKNN a few years later; it had two six-cylinder engines called Gypsy queens, two sets of wings and could carry eight parachutists and their kit to 13,000ft.

It was a sunny but cloudy day when we took off and climbed for an hour, looking down I could not see the ground at all, there was complete cloud cover. On take-off I estimated the base of the cloud at 3,000ft. Remember I had never seen a French altimeter before.

After about fifty minutes the instructor said to me, "Monsieur Green, Mont Blanc," and pointed out of the window at a snow-covered mountain top that was poking up out of the clouds? I thought, bloody hell, they are going to chuck me out of here, I cannot see though the cloud and it seemed there were mountains somewhere below. I was contemplating smashing into a mountain at 120 miles an hour Then he opened the door and a chap stepped out without a word; and the door was closed, 'blimey'. Then he called me.

He said to me, "OK straight free-fall no manoeuvres". He opened the door; I knew that I had to go at that precise moment to land on the airfield that is if the pilot had calculated his position correctly. I stepped out alone into the freezing air. My brain was racing; I knew that in the Second World War the Americans had flown the Army Parachutists into Sicily and; due to clouds had dropped them into the sea, poor devils.

Quickly adopting a free-fall position; looking like a frog; I do not mean looking like a Frenchman. I mean arms and legs akimbo, elbows bent, knees bent, and this creates a shuttle-cock effect which is stable and keeps you face to earth. They held this smaller tight position because they found they could manoeuvre faster, unlike in the UK and America where they spread their arms and legs wide.

There was no view, just a complete carpet of white cloud far below. I decided I would open my chute as I entered the cloud just in case the base had lowered; you see I did not trust the altimeter, which was in metres. I knew that I had left the plane at around 12,000ft (it was 2,500metres).

That gave me a full minute of falling free; it might seem strange to you, but I got bored. I had done some trampoline practise in previous years. I thought, I'll practise a back somersault, I know he said no manoeuvres, but nobody can see me. Shoving my hands forward further into the 120mph slipstream I flipped over backwards to face the sky!

Waaah! There was a bloody great eagle about to grab me with his out-stretched talons. Face to face with his big yellow-orange eyes. I curled up into a ball in fear which caused me to tumble and increase my downward speed.

Then a realization that it was an instructor that had followed me out of the plane and had slip-streamed me, that is he was so close behind me that it caused a vacuum that kept him there with hardly any effort and of course study my expertise. He would have been quite able to grab me at any time should I have got into difficulties, even pulling my ripcord as a last resort. Why did I think he was an eagle?

He was wearing a dark coloured jumpsuit and parachute, black tight-fitting gloves; He held his fingers in a claw-like position probably to gain more air resistance. Wearing a brown leather helmet used by cyclists that had rolls of leather running front to back, with the bubble eyed dark yellow goggles, his head definitely looked like an eagle's head. To say his rather large nose looked like a beak would be unkind, so I won't say it.

Recovering stability in seconds I rolled over to look at him again, using my hands in the slipstream as paddles. But he was gone, roll again, spin, no-one, tantalizing, amazing! Did I imagine him?

I opened my chute on entering the cloud, drifting out of the cloud base at about 2,000ft. Bloody hell; there he was standing on the landing site, a pit of shingle, and a red cross to aim for. He was signalling with his arms, left a bit, a bit more, I landed right on target.

Think about it, the Pilot's great navigation over thick cloud before they had satellite navigation. A free-fall of a mile through cloud and the instructor that scared me, standing on the target with his chute off! He did not know that he scared me witless. Boy! I got a severe telling off, "If you do not do as you are told, you go home". He had disappeared from my sight by assuming a head down position which increased his descent speed and had opened his chute at a much lower altitude than 2000ft, in order to direct me to the target, apparently there was a bonus system at work. It had taken a year to do thirty-two jumps in England, partly due to weather and shortage of suitable aircraft. Here I did six jumps that first day, all from 12,000ft.

Another reason was that in the UK, too much time was spent looking at weather forecasts and calculating wind speed against the speed of the aircraft being used, a lot of good opportunities were missed. What surprised me was that the French did use an anemometer to check the wind-speed but instead of calculations they threw a toilet roll out of the plane after take-off at around 2,000ft to simulate a parachute's drift.

I completed my course and on return to the UK started British Skydiving Ltd and started using the French techniques at Thruxton. In the photo below the Chief Instructor is wearing a striped shirt I am at the top right.

Something that I realized in France was that you could not run a parachute club with a committee. It needed one boss, one leader as it was done at Chalon-sur-Soane but that was military with an officer in charge. I would do it privately with a limited company.

FRENCH MILITARY SKYDIVING SCHOOL

Looking at this photograph made me realize that I never saw any ladies skydiving, perhaps they were part of the administration team.

INSTRUCTORS LICENCE

15th JANUARY 1960
The examiners were Peter Lang and Mike Reilly. After dispatching Peter and Mike at Stapleford Tawney Aerodrome I passed to receive my licence. Students were not allowed to jump this day because the wind was about 30mph.

KIDLINGTON AIRPORT

5th JUNE 1960

In the above photo I am standing with Martin Griffiths and Mike Browsinski. I regret I cannot name the others. We hired a Tiger Moth G-AMEY and a Tripacer G-ARCA.

We had all done our basic training at Fairoaks. Mike Browsinski went through the hangar roof at Fairoaks and luckily ended sitting across a steel beam, otherwise he would have fallen about 40ft.

JUMP INTO A RUBBISH DUMP

31st August 1960.

Mike Reilly, Martin Griffiths and I did a display at Biggin Hill for an Australian television company. We used a De-Havilland Rapide G-ANYD piloted by K. Sirrett. I took the club advertising caravan and it created a lot of interest with its display of parachute equipment and the offer of weekend training courses.

The first jump was from 6,500ft and I was spotter and first out. All went well but on the next jump which was my 60th jump I ended up covered in household rubbish. We jumped from 4,500ft but the spot was not good (not me). In free-fall I tracked like a swallow to get across the sky but when I opened my chute I knew I was doomed to land by the housing estate on the west of the field, Martin was close by. The airfield is on a hill and now I could see a deep valley on the west side which was being filled with house-hold garbage by the council. I had the choice of housing or rubbish dump; I chose the dump as I could see wires stretched across the gaps in the housing. Martin chose the estate and landed on a road.

I hit the top of the heap and tumbled head over heels down the rubbish to the bottom of the heap. I was covered in smelly rubbish, but happy to be alive.

I clambered up to the top of the rubbish heap and rolled the chute up in a bundle and we caught a bus back to the main entrance of the airfield. I was happy to be smelly and not dead. There was nobody working at the dump and nobody had inquired if we were safe when we went missing which is a bit strange. The other two guys managed to land safely on the west side of the airfield.

You might like to know that the Insurance in case we landed on someone or damaged something was two shillings and six pence. 12.5pence in today's money.

BIGGIN HILL

17th SEPTEMBER 1960

On the 17th September 1960 I jumped at Biggin Hill again with Mike Reilly, Dave Hall and Martin Griffiths. We hired a De-Havilland Rapide but only jumped from 2,200ft and I used my 20ft GQ parachute,

Martin landed heavily, lost a tooth and had concussion. I did not see Martin much after this as he became an airline pilot. This was followed by building and opening a brewery and a restaurant in Herefordshire. The last time I saw him was in May 1980 when I married my 2nd wife 'Peggy'.

KIDLINGTON (OXFORD)

5th OCTOBER 1960

Before I settled to run the club at Thruxton our group used to travel every weekend to try different airfields and aircraft. We went to Kidlington airfield near Oxford a few times. Kidlington airfield was established in 1935 and was an RAF base in WW2. By 1970 it was the 2nd busiest private airfield in the UK. When we were there in the early 1960's there were only a few Tripacer planes and always a very relaxed atmosphere. These aircraft could carry three skydivers to about 7,000ft. altitude in a reasonable time and cost, having a high wing it was good for spotting and dropping students with a static line. We packed our parachutes on the grass in front of the control tower. It was a large grass airfield with fields outside the boundaries.

To give you an idea of size it is now called London Oxford Airport and there is now an asphalt runway 5,092ft long. There were some wartime wooden huts scattered on the south side near the club house, now in that area are huge aircraft hangars.

THE PICNIC

05th JUNE 1960   KIDLINGTON.

On this day three of us jumped from 8,500ft. Stan Anstee the BPA treasurer was the spotter. When we left the plane, we were too far North over the cabbage fields so I got into a delta wing position and flew towards the A 4095 road on the West side where I could thumb a lift back to the airfield entrance gate.

The road was not busy and there was a very large grass verge. I could see a family of four sitting round a chequered tablecloth having a picnic. They never heard me coming and I did not call out, I landed right beside them and after a parachute roll ended sitting beside the wife. She had an orange juice in her hand and she immediately offered it to me with a shocked look on her face.

The husband asked, "Where has your plane crashed?" They did not seem to believe that I had left an aircraft voluntarily. The little boy with big eyes never spoke. After drinking tea and eating cake they gave me a lift back to the Airfield control tower. Stan was still missing so we went looking for him, the ground was hard, and he got knocked out. We could not find him as he was amongst the cabbages, Stan took over an hour to walk back at the airport.

SLEEVES

25th SEPT 1960

On this day was my first jump with a parachute sleeve that I manufactured. I used it on my GQ 20ft red and white quartered canopy No 352206. I jumped from 4,000 over Shoreham Airfield.

In my Logbook, I wrote; *Packed sleeve, first time really scared, knees like jelly. Really pleased. Such a gentle deployment. 66th Jump.*

WHERE'S THE BODY?

1960.

I did sigh well after I did a parachute jump at Sywell Aerodrome, Near Northampton in the UK during the 1960s. I had been parachuting and skydiving for two years when Pat Slattery and I decided to go to Sywell to jump. We enjoyed going to different aerodromes for a number of reasons. The travelling, jumping from different aircraft and most of all I enjoyed looking at the scenery as I fell through the sky.

Only it did not feel like falling until this particular day. It feels like floating on a soft cushion. It's like you are lying on a cushion of air. The countryside below looks like a huge fruit bowl below you from 6,000ft up.

The fruit bowl below with its hedges, Copses and different coloured small fields never failed to amaze me. There is nothing like England for shades of green. As you free-fall it appears that you are descending into and below the rim of that bowl, if you are not carrying an altimeter this means you should be getting ready to open your chute. The only time you get a sensation of your speed is when you pass down the side of a cloud. I remember when I first passed through a cumulus cloud and flinched because it looked hard, but you do not feel it. All you get is moisture collecting on your face.

This day I would experience speed and fear. Sywell aerodrome was a vast expanse of grass but it is not flat. When you view from the Control Tower area the land rises, it is not a hill but just a bump in the terrain. There was no reason to alter our altimeters as we would open our chutes above 1,500ft. It was a cloudless summer day; the aircraft was a Cessna.

Pat and I wanted to spot for ourselves, that is direct the pilot to the exit point which we estimated would allow our drifting to land where we would not have to walk a long way to get a cup of tea.

I left the plane at 7,000ft, I had previously been using a standard 28ft GQ parachute and this was before the use of sleeves which enclosed the canopy to reduce the opening shock. The opening shock of an un-sleeved parachute at terminal velocity (over 120mph) kept bruising my body and if I wore a string vest it looked as if I had a fishnet tattoo. The large harness buckle on the British chutes bruised my chest so often I had to have a Mastectomy operation, no not vasectomy. Yes, I know women have Mastectomies. I felt and looked as though Shylock had taken his pound of flesh.

This day I was using my brand-new orange and white quartered parachute purchased from The GQ

Parachute Company. The attraction of this chute was that it had been designed for pilot ejection from high speed aircraft. Jet planes were getting faster and Jet pilots parachutes were being blown to shreds by the opening shock. This chute was designed to open slowly. It would stream out and remain in what was often described as a candle shape. '

So often with early pioneers chutes they streamed out and never opened and as they were white it was described as a candle. This new design would remain in a candle effect until the drag caused a reduction in speed then it would open slowly at first then snap open. It was smooth and graceful as opposed to the brutal shocks that I had previously experienced, with an old army style chute. At Shoreham it caused one of my boots to come off, I never found it.

I really enjoyed this free-fall, trying out aerobatic manoeuvres, viewing the countryside, feeling the rush of warm air pummelling my cheeks. I looked at my altimeter. I had got carried away and had gone below 2,000ft. On reaching for my ripcord, which should have been in an elasticated pocket on the left of my chest. I could not feel it, I looked for it.
'It was not there', The handle had come out of the housing.

I had ten seconds to live. I turned my attention to operate the reserve chute clipped to the harness on front of my chest. This was a 24ft parachute that I had to open and throw into the slipstream. As my hands closed over the reserve it caused me to roll over onto my back and that made the main ripcord to come floating over my shoulder from where it had been hiding! Ah, I thought I would rather descend on the main chute and grabbed the ripcord and pulled.

As the parachute streamed out, I thought, 'OH NO! That was a big mistake'. I had wasted three seconds. Now I had 7seconds or less to live. But I had not been counting; I probably had about 3seconds to live.

Most accidents are not caused by a single action or inaction. They are usually caused by a combination of events. I had seen a parachutist's death caused by him getting too engrossed in aerobatic activities, then getting too low. *One of his hands was smaller than the other, so he wore large gloves.* Then his rather large gloves which helped in skydiving manoeuvres impeded him opening the reserve chute. He might have survived but for the high beech trees.

Now feeling secure that my chute was going to open I looked down. **At that split second; all I could see was part of a hedge, a grass verge and the edge of a road. I could even see the blades of grass!** There was no time for thought. My whole body cramped up and I retched violently at the same moment!

Then a strange sense of peace and quiet came over me and I thought I was in heaven.
I opened my eyes and found I was standing upright on the grass verge outside the airfield hedge, I am not dead. I had landed on my feet and did not even fall over. I unclipped the harness and stood beside the empty road, I took off my helmet and overalls and threw them on the grass, the sun was hot, and life felt wonderful.

I considered what had happened, the final opening of the chute had caused a bounce by the stretching of the nylon suspension cords, it was at that precise point my feet touched the ground without any impact. I did have a guardian angel. Pat Slattery was unaware of what had happened for he was floating down to the airfield.

A 7cwt white van came hurtling up the road and stopped beside me, the driver jumped out and walked past me. He looked around at the scene of discarded parachutes and helmet then turned to me and asked, "Where's the body"? "What body," I asked; obviously my euphoria had stopped me thinking. "The body of the parachutist, his chute did not open" he said.

"That is me" I replied. He looked at me in a very strange way, then without a word got in the van and drove away. He must have thought I was Mr Cool, but I think I was in shock.

I was on the opposite side of a field from the control tower. I think this narrow road led to Sywell Grange which is north of the Airfield. From the viewpoint of the control tower, I had disappeared behind the rising ground as or before the chute opened. Eventually Pat came and collected me. This event did not put me off as I continued to Skydive and soon opened the first skydiving school in the UK at Thruxton.

I do have the feeling that I am alive today because before I started parachuting, I read all the books on the subject including all the guys that experimented with fixed wings, most of those guys died in entanglements. The moment any panic sets in you are lost.

SKYDIVING EQUIPMENT 1960'S

By this time, we were using American surplus military parachutes which we modified ourselves simply with the use of a razor blade. The parachutes were in pristine condition because they had never been used. It was an established rule of law in the American military establishment to discard or sell off parachutes after ten years whether they had been used or had remained in sealed metal drums.

I was manufacturing sleeves for skydivers that owned an assortment of British and foreign parachutes.

The purpose of these sleeves was that the sleeve enclosed the canopy while it was deploying which resulted in less tangle and reduced the violent opening shock of coming to a quick stop at hundred and twenty miles per hour. The reason being that as a sleeve was pulled off the main chute by the sprung drogue parachute it slowed the opening.

Prior to using this system, it left the imprint of your underwear on the torso especially if you were wearing string vests. It created so many bruises on my right nipple that I ended up having a mastectomy; I know that is normally a woman's problem, but it was my breast not a vasectomy. "Just a little cut", they said. When I woke up there were so many bandages, I thought they had mummified me, but Shylock had taken his pound of flesh; and happily, the tumour did not regrow.

On a trip to London's East End rag trade warehouses to purchase rolls of high-quality cotton cloth, I asked if they ever got parachutes. The chap opened a green steel drum and there was a most wonderful sight; an olive-green American back-pack parachute. I knew from magazines that it was a B4 back-pack with a C9 orange and white 28-foot Ripstop nylon canopy inside the pack. "How much?" I asked while thinking that on 15th May 1959, my British parachute had cost me over £200. "How about £8?" he asked. I kicked the parachute over with my boot to show that

I did not think much of it and offered £5. "OK, he said and asked how many I wanted to take?" "You might as well fill the van," I told him. My van was a brand-new Volkswagen with a 1,600cc engine. I drove home so blinking fast over that 45 miles that I blew up one of the four cylinders. Undeterred I drove straight back to London for a second load with the engine firing on three cylinders; an amazing engine. These parachutes were the basis and backbone of the British Skydiving Ltd School.

The parachutes were cheap enough to experiment on, so with a razor blade I cut out four panels down the angled seams. It looked like two figure L's at the rear of the chutes. This produced two effects; it gave the parachute a forward speed which a standard chute did not have. Secondly, by tying handles and cords to the outside suspension lines of the outer openings it enabled the parachutist to rotate the parachute.

This was a most desirable modification for the parachutist; for then he could see where he was going, enjoy a view of 360 degrees, fly the chute away from trees and power lines and, best of all, turn into the wind to reduce the landing speed. I fixed D ring shackles to the harness to fit the reserve and I retailed these modified parachutes at £53 each and hired them out to Club Members at £1 per jump with the packers getting ten shillings. That is 50 pence to you.

THE AUSTER INCIDENT

25th SEPT 1960. SHOREHAM

There was no established system to hire an aircraft for parachuting. We would tout around for any owner to fly us and we would pay the costs. On this day, my friend Pat Slattery was with me and we obtained the services of a young lady that owned an Auster. For those that have not seen an Auster, it is a delightful aircraft, quite old even then in the 1960s. It has a metal frame covered in a linen fabric; high wings and can carry a pilot plus three or only two parachutists due to the weight of their kit. They were used in WW2 to ferry agents across the English Channel.

The pilot usually prepares the Aircraft for the parachutists but as this was her first time to drop parachutists, we did it. We took the starboard door off to enable our exit. The door is quite large to enable entry to the rear passenger seats. With the door off it makes it much easier to exit the aircraft and allows the parachutists to guide the pilot to the upwind exit point.
Pat climbed into the rear seat; I sat in front next to the pilot. We climbed to 4,000ft and turned into wind. I had asked the pilot to throttle back on my signal to enable an easier exit from the aircraft; the exit position was still above the airfield because the wind was very light.

On my signal she cut the throttle and I swung my legs out, putting my feet on the wing strut. At the same moment the aircraft went into a vertical dive with the engine screaming like a WW2 STUKA dive bomber; I just wanted to get out the door, but I was stuck there. Pat was beating me with his fists and pushing hard to get me out of the door and release him from the metal cage that was surrounding him and hurtling towards the ground.

I was looking straight down at the airfield through the whirling propeller. For a second I thought about being chopped up by the prop and slamming into the ground. Then Pat pulled me back into the plane like a doll or the dummy that I was; the pilot pulled out of the dive, there was very little height left, she turned and landed.

We would not have survived had we chosen a lower exit height. The reason for the near disaster; The Aircraft had been fitted with dual controls; there was a joystick on my side of the plane. I was sitting further back than a passenger would and the joystick operated freely until I swung out, then my parachute pack slammed the stick forward against the control panel causing the dive.
The pilot could not pull her control stick back until Pat saw the problem and with his strong arms pulled me back into the rear of the plane. The pilot bravely

took us up again after a cup of coffee and of course after removing the second joystick, it was no longer considered to be called a JOY-stick.

We were then able to enjoy the pleasure of floating down looking at the Sussex scenery with the Abbey on the hillside and across the sea towards the Isle of Wight. A bit of danger does add spice to life. Perhaps the reason I did not realize the danger of the joystick was because I was fascinated by the scenery and busy shipping activities in the Port of Shoreham. And all our previous pilots had removed the control stick themselves. Accidents and incidents like this are hardly ever because of one simple error or reason. They are usually a combination of two or three errors. This will become apparent in other stories and tragedies that I will relate.

SKYDIVING IN STYLE.

RAF Mildenhall in Suffolk, England, was the base of 7513th Tactical Group of the United States Air Forces in Europe. Unfortunately, my parachuting logbook for the period was lost but it was in the 1960s that I received a telephone call at the office of British Skydiving Ltd at The Toll House, Runfold, Farnham in Surrey. (*Now a private dwelling*) It was an Officer of the USAF at Mildenhall and he asked if I could supply two Skydivers for the next Air Show at the base which was only a couple of weeks away. I said yes and he asked where the nearest airfield to my residence was, I told him Fairoaks Aerodrome, Nr Woking, Surrey. He said he would send an aircraft to collect us on the day before the show.

A member of my sky-diving club, Sherdy Vatsndal agreed to come with me and on the Saturday afternoon we arrived at Fairoaks to find a beautiful Military Beaver Aircraft waiting for us. We even got a salute from the pilot. Without any consultations we were whisked away and after a wonderful flight skirting around the North of London we landed at Mildenhall where a staff car was waiting for us at the side of the peri-track.

We were driven to the Officers' quarters.
I noticed that the car engine was running while we disembarked from the beaver and the driver always left the engine running. When I asked him why he said that he was instructed to leave it running as starting the engine caused more wear than when it was running continuously. I thought this rather odd. It might apply in a sub-zero climate, but I thought it a waste of petrol.

We dined in the Officers Mess and were amazed at the choice of food available and the huge portions which meant the plates were twice the size of the dinner plates that I used in my café. We went to bed early and again at breakfast there was a stunning array of food.

I was surprized at the mixture and quantity being consumed of juices, cereals, steaks with two eggs sunny side up on top, followed by pancakes. No wonder those guys were all very large. I had always been brought up to eat everything on my plate and still do, even when the food is free and self-service, I never put more than I can eat on my plate. Perhaps it is due to being a child in the 2nd world war does that. Nearly all the Americans in the self-service restaurant had steaks that they took two bites from and just dipped into the yolks of their two eggs. The amount of food left on the plates astonished me.

We all assembled in the briefing room. At the British Air-shows someone would say to the skydivers something like this. "After the Stampe aircraft has finished his aerobatics you drop in on your chutes, OK, chaps." Here we listened to a programme run second by second with talk of the jet fighters starting their approach run from Swansea in Wales passing over the airfield at Mach 1.

It was not very comforting to hear that we were to jump from 12,000 ft. as those fighters were approaching at the speed of sound. After we were asked how long we would be in free-fall and how long under the canopy we would be, we were given a time to exit the Beaver aircraft at a number of minutes and seconds past the hour. Then the briefing officer said, "The time is," and everybody held up their left arms and adjusted their chronometers. I never owned a wristwatch; I still do not wear one as for some reason I cannot stand having anything on my wrist. But I held my arm up to be in with the crowd, Sherdy also held up his arm as he had a watch, but it did not have a second hand on it!

The next hours are a blur but now we are at 12,000ft in the Beaver aircraft cruising round in a circle waiting for the time to drop which we had agreed with the pilot to give us the signal to go. It was so pleasant lying on the floor with our heads out the doorway watching the air-show from above. The airfield was covered with helicopters all buzzing around at a low altitude playing some sort of war game when the pilot shouted "GO" I thought, Bloody hell this is dangerous, I am going to get minced up by those helicopter blades. But the brain works at enormous speed in these situations and I debated the issues like this. I have got to go now as there are two fighter jets coming here at Mach1. I do not wish to meet them in the air. I will jump and if those helicopters are still below me, I will open slightly higher and drift off to the side of the airfield.

I jumped and Sherdy followed. I must say I did not look at the view as my eyes were glued on those helicopters and my brain was saying mincemeat-mincemeat. After falling for 30seconds and we were about 6,000ft the helicopters dispersed to the corners of the field. Now that was organization, at the British shows it might be 10 minutes between events.

Now perfectly relaxed we landed, but as our chutes slowly collapsed to the ground there was an almighty Ka-boom, Ka-Boom as the two fighter jets broke the speed of sound over the airfield and we watched their blazing red-blue exhausts disappear over the countryside at about 500ft above the ground.
Could those pilots see us as they approached? No, we would not have shown on their radar at all as even Hot-air balloons with their propane tanks do not show up very well. Since then I have had military fighter pilots line up on me in my balloon, they later told me we were very difficult to locate.

We were then again whisked away by car to the restaurant for a coffee, tea or Coca Cola and choice from piles of pies, pasties apple pies and pastries or donut, muffin, cake, Cheesecake, fruit pie with ice cream or custard. I was in the British Air force for a month before I got chucked out because I was dyslexic, also I was in the British Army for three years and I never ever saw food like that except the Army boxers got steaks for some reason.

After our tea and cake, Notice the singular (cake) we were driven to the Beaver Aircraft and flown back to Fairoaks Aerodrome before it got dark. This was truly an adventure into the unknown and an interesting look into how the other side live. Americans are not just English-speaking people that live over the water they are completely different in many ways.

Sherdy Vatsndal and I are standing by the American Air Force 'Beaver' aircraft that flew us to Mildenhall and back to Fairoaks aerodrome.

Sherdy died in his sleep when he was still a very young and super-fit guy.

SKYDIVING, THE BLACK HOLE

18th SEPTEMBER 1960
And a question about my sanity

I took a team of skydivers from the club at Thruxton to jump at Weston Aerodrome in Ireland. This was on 18th September 1960; six of us were to jump from a Rapide at 12,000ft. It had been estimated that there were 25,000 people in the crowd watching us.

We exited the plane in a group, looking down; it all looked rather brown. I think everyone wore brown clothes and cloth caps in those days. Then apparently a commentator told them to look up.

The whole perimeter changed to white and yellow as if a field of daises had turned their heads to the sun. Ah, I thought, all those people watching, waiting to see the chutes eventually open. No! They are not. They want to see them fail. People go to car races, not to see cars driving boringly round and round, they want bashes, exciting crashes.

Then I saw what appeared to be a very black round disk on the ground. It was like looking down a gun barrel, an intense black. Then I realized it was a very large factory chimney stack.

Interestingly, I lined my-self up over it. I thought, I could fall straight down that chimney; that would delight the crowd. I kept manoeuvring over the black hole; *I will go straight down that chimney; that will excite the crowd.* I was not contemplating suicide, I love life. All I wanted to do was entertain the crowd. The speed in free-fall is approximately 120 mph; I was less than eight seconds away from death.

I woke up, part of my brain questioned, "What are you doing". I immediately pulled my ripcord and drifted down onto the airfield, job done. I never told anyone, family, friends, or enemies.

I understand that early fighter pilots had a problem when firing at targets like boats trains and buildings; they would fly straight into them quite accidently; they only did that once. There was a saying for it "Target fixation". I was certainly fixated on that black Chimney flue. Oh, there was one chap I told after I retired; Pat Slattery. He was a very active skydiver. He told me that he had had similar thoughts on an air display that he had helped to organize.

Unfortunately Pat died a few years later because he sky-dived from high altitude and did a scuba dive the same day. He died from the bends, air bubbles in the blood, he was an interesting character. He was from the east end of London. My daughter's second name is Patricia after him. My daughter Helen Patricia did one skydive from 13,000ft in Spain, there was a film made and it shows that she was perfectly relaxed during the one minute of free-fall, actually laughing and looking around at the scenery. She was fearless when riding sidecar in International Motorbike Trials, that's my girl.

FAI LICENCE

13th OCTOBER1960 I received my FAI parachute certificate A and B. No 57 Signed by Lord Brabazon
Cert A = 10 jumps.
Cert B= 25Free-fall jumps, including 15 over 10seconds, 5 of 20seconds, and one of 30seconds with ability to hold heading and stop a spin.

GREEN FLYER

12th APRIL 1962

My favourite modification for students was an American Army camouflaged 28ft canopy which I cut out a pyramid shape centrally and two L shapes for turning the chute. The centre opening gave a good driving force. Whenever I cut or modified a parachute canopy, I tested it my-self. I found this design one of the best in respect of handling and safety.

THE GREENFLYER

THE PERSISTANT ASSISTANT

JUNE 1960. KIDLINGTON (OXFORD)

As I was and still am dyslexic and had never typed until 2009 when I discovered Microsoft Word. I employed a part time assistant and bookkeeper to help with the accounts of Alf's Café, at Runfold, the typing for the BPA when I was the Secretary, and the British Skydiving Ltd accounts.

Her name was Pamela and she lived in our village. She was constantly saying she wanted to parachute. She was physically fit but as she had children, I did not wish to see her hurt. Any injury could affect her income because she also worked for others. She obtained the required paperwork, but I still said no. But prior to our next visit to Kidlington she nagged and nagged me until I reluctantly agreed.

She had received all the training required not only from me but others. I took her up, just the pilot, me and her in a 1958 Piper PA-20 Tripacer. It was perfect weather with a very light wind which would take her drifting away from the buildings towards the A4095 on the east side.

I took her to an altitude of 3000ft instead of the 2000ft normally used for static line students. Perhaps I had better explain. My friends and I when we trained as students, used to jump from the plane at 1,500ft and count one, two, three seconds. Then we had to pull the ripcord which opened the parachute pack, a little parachute with a spring in it popped out like a jack-in–the box and pulled the 28ft main chute out into the slipstream.

With a Static line, the static line was secured to the plane and after the student had fallen 20ft it pulled the pack open and then pulled the main chute out until a break tie broke and the chute would start to deploy. If anything went wrong the student had a 24ft reserve chute attached to the front of the harness which they had to open and deploy.

Pamela was in good spirits as we climbed to altitude, the slipstream was pleasantly warm. She sat at the door with her knees pulled up and her arms around her knees. It was too noisy to talk. She was watching the scenery unfold and lost in her thoughts.

The point of exit was approaching I told her to swing her legs out the door, she did not move. I thought she had not heard, I shouted and repeated my instruction, she ignored me. I must admit I lost my temper and in a moment of madness I put my hands under her legs and back, lifted her up and dropped her out of the door. I watched with trepidation, the fall of 20ft seemed to take a lifetime. The canopy opened and I sighed in relief.

As the plane descended circling around her I noticed she was not steering the chute, her arms were hanging loosely by her side. I asked the pilot to land near her as she approached the western boundary, this he did, and I ran towards her as she landed by a metal fence. She was sitting with her back pressed to the fence as she watched me approach then said, "That was wonderful, I turned this way and that using the toggles."

At that moment she wondered what she was leaning against and turned to look. She never knew the fence was there. I knew that she had not steered the parachute and I know she was not aware that I dropped her out of the plane. Had the main chute failed I realized for that she might not have operated the reserve chute.

She never asked to jump again and ten years later she married my father and gave me a beautiful sister. I am so pleased she survived but it shows that some people switch off mentally when under stress which can be fatal.

BRITISH PARACHUTE ASSOCIATION

THE DAY OF FOUNDING.

22nd OCTOBER 1960 (Saturday)

I met in a London coffee bar with friends on the 22nd September1960 to consider the formation of a Parachute association. G.H. (Herb) Hoeschle President of The Parachute Club of Canada was there to provide advice. He and his wife were on holiday in the UK. Mike Reilly proposed setting up The British Parachute Association. Within minutes it was agreed that he was Chairman, I was the Secretary and Stanley Anstee was responsible for the accounts, my wife Ann was there to take notes.

Now it is a highly organised association responsible for the safe operation of Parachuting and Skydiving in this country. Below is a photograph of this momentous meeting taken in the coffee bar below.

Mike Reilly is at the centre of the photo. I am on his left side and my 1st wife Ann is on his right.
G. H. (Herb) Hoeschle is on the front left with his wife and Stan Anstee and wife on the right.

I cannot remember where the meeting was
but it might have been near the London School of
Economics as Mike was studying there at Houghton
Street, Holborn. Or quite likely the coffee bar might
have been near the Holborn Underground Station.

This was the first wonderful logo for the BPA. It was designed and created by Fred Gayler. I like the simplicity and the fact that it explains all the features of Skydiving in one go.

I met Fred when we were parachuting at Fairoaks Aerodrome. But lost touch with him after we spent a week at Sandown Airport on the Isle of Wight learning to Skydive in July 1959.

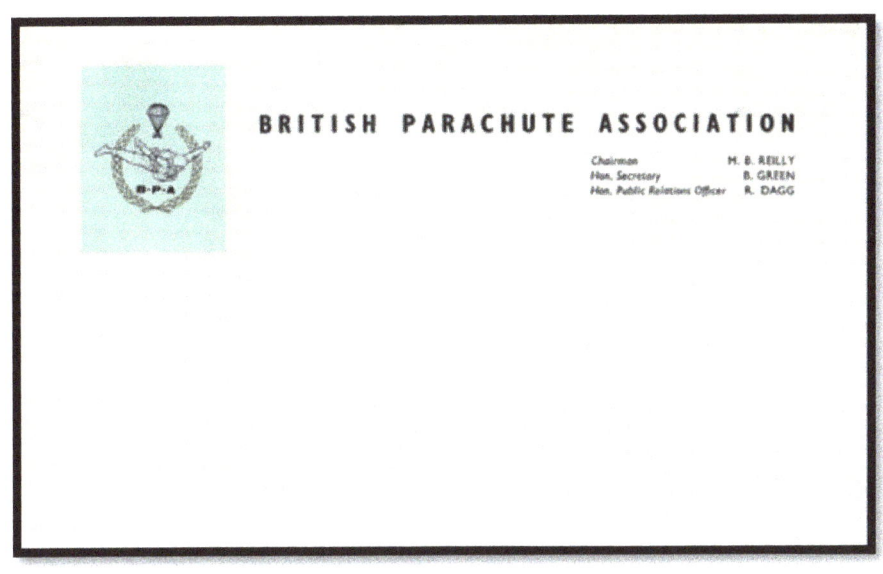

BPA HEADED NOTE PAPER

BRITISH PARACHUTE ASSOCIATION AND ROYAL AERO CLUB PANEL OF PARACHUTING EXAMINERS.
Undated but lists
M. B. REILLY, P. LANG. J.T. BASNETT.

BRITISH PARACHUTE ASSOCIATION
HON. SECRETARY B. GREEN.
"WILMSLOW" RUNFOLD, NR FARNHAM, SURREY.

'WILMSLOW'

There are numerous letters from The Royal Aero club forwarded to my residence at "Wilmslow" to answer as Secretary of the B.P.A. dated 23rd November 1960 to 24th April 1961

That is my 1955 Triumph Bonneville JHN 939 standing there. I write about adrenaline rush later when talking about the members of the Skydiving fraternity.

I sold 'Wilmslow' in 1970 and it is now a private residence.

THE DARK SIDE

Before I settled to run the club at Thruxton our group used to travel every weekend to try different airfields and aircraft. We went to Kidlington airfield near Oxford a few times. This airfield was established in 1935 and was an RAF base in WW2. By 1970 it was the 2nd busiest private airfield in the UK. But when we were there in the early 1960's there were only a few Tripacer planes and always a very relaxed atmosphere. These aircraft could carry three skydivers to about 7,000ft. altitude in a reasonable time and cost, having a high wing it was good for spotting and dropping students with a static line.

We packed our parachutes on the grass in front of the control tower. It was a large grass airfield with fields outside the boundaries. To give you an idea of size it is now called London Oxford Airport and there is now an asphalt runway 5,092ft long.

There were some wartime wooden huts scattered on the south side near the club house, now in that area are huge aircraft hangars.

FALLING OUT OVER SHOES

MAY 1961

It was in May 1961 that I went with Mike Reilly, Martin Griffiths to Sywell Aerodrome in Northamptonshire in order to Skydive. I say Skydive as opposed to Parachute because to parachute is a term used if you operate the parachute in order to leave an aircraft and arrive safely on the ground. Skydiving means there is the added attraction of doing aerobatic movements without the fear of landing badly on the Gymnasium mat or doing a belly flop in the water as the result of a bad dive.

To Skydive means flying as high as you can and delaying the opening of the parachute to enjoy the wonderful feeling of falling or even the sensation of flying when placing your body into a delta wing shape and seeing the ground pass underneath you.

These days fabric wings are being used which extends the flying time considerably, they are being nicknamed the flying squirrels. My emblem for the British Skydiving Club was a flying squirrel. It is an unfortunate fact that most of the early pioneers that used wings of cloth or solid wings died while trying out their wings.

On arrival at Sywell Aerodrome we hired a Piper PA22-150 Tripacer This aircraft had a Four-cylinder Lycoming 0-320B. It had high fabric wings that were supported by a "V" strut that attached forward and level with the door. It was a four-seater, but we removed the two rear seats and the door on the port side. We asked the pilot to fly as high as he could in one hour. This Aircraft was produced between 1950 to 1964 and the climb rate was supposed to be 800ft per minute, with a cruise speed of 134mph a stall speed of 49mph and a ceiling of 16,500ft. We would not be going above 12,000ft because there is always a danger of blackouts from lack of oxygen. We asked him to fly as high as he could, we did not ask him to circle the aerodrome.

The sky was clear but there was a chill in the air, we had the RAF thin flying suits on over our normal clothes. We sat on the bare aluminium floor behind the pilot, Mike got in first, I think he knew it was going to be draughty, I sat in the middle and Martin sat at the door to do the spotting and direct the plot to the required exit point over the airfield.

I felt quite cosy at first sitting in between them. We sat in silence because of the engine noise and the wind howling round the cabin, it was getting very cold and the plane was not climbing very well with the pilot and three kitted out skydivers on board. It was taking a long time to get the height. Martin kept poking his head out the door to check on the wind direction by looking at clues like the airfield windsock and smoke from chimneys. I thought he was also looking at the views.

Suddenly without a word or gesture he rolled out the door, I had this done to me before as a strange joke, the joker leaving others in the plane causing them to miss the drop zone target. I was not going to fall for that trick, so I quickly rolled out the door after him. This caused me to tumble and I found my-self on my back looking at the plane. At that moment Mike's hands; then head and shoulders came diving out the doorway. To my amazement his right hand then shot out and grabbed the wing-strut and he hung on like a trapeze artist, so I stayed falling on my back to watch what he was up to.

I was not surprised at his speed of movement or agility because he was a superb athlete. I saw the plane veer violently to the left in a semi-circle before the pilot recovered and flew off with Mike still hanging on below the wing, what puzzled me was why he doing it?

I now had to turn my attention to what I was doing so I rolled over. Below me Martin was in free-fall still and to my horror below him was a great big town, it was Northampton. There were no open spaces to head for, so it was pointless to open high and hope to drift away from the housing estates and huge expanse of glass roofed shoe factories that appeared to be everywhere below us.

I opened my chute as I saw Martin going for his ripcord, thankfully the wind was light and we both had steerable 7TU chutes. With razor blades we had cut out five narrow panels at the back of the chutes and at each end a large cut which enabled us to turn the parachute around in order to see where we were going this also gave a forward speed of about 5mph.

I saw Martin land successfully on a road in a housing estate, I was still over an enormous factory with a glass roof. I had heard that shoe factories in Northampton had glass roof's, but it has a different effect on the mind when you think you might be visiting them through the roof. I managed to land in the front executive car park but left part of my parachute on the roof, (the sleeve that encased the canopy to reduce the opening shock.) I did not bother to retrieve it for I could not imagine anyone climbing forty feet up over glass to get it for me.

I walked over the road to Martin who explained that he got so cold' and stiff he fell out the door of the plane, I replied that we were both lucky that we did not go through one of those glass factory roofs and end up as cold stiffs.

We got a taxi back to the airfield where Mike was waiting for us and over a cup of coffee, he explained that as his head cleared the door, he saw the town and grabbed the strut. Then he held on for over two minutes while the pilot flew back to Sywell Aerodrome; that was nearly five miles at 130 mph in a chilly wind.

I believe that the area that Martin and I landed in was Moulton Park. That is not a wooded grassy park but a dense housing and business estate.

R.A.F WETHERSFIELD

17th JUNE 1961

Display at R.A.F. 20th Tactical Unit, Wethersfield, myself Mike Reilly, Tony Miller, Stan Anstee and Martin Griffith's.

We flew in a De Havilland Rapide AFNH Piloted by Ken Syrett. There was a crowd estimated at 50,000. We all landed nicely in front of the crowd. Martin threw his reserve and descended on both. I used my GQ 20ft Red/White chute.

I mention in my records that we were allowed to look inside a Vulcan bomber.

NOVEMBER 1961.

COLONEL DARE WILSON the CHAIRMAN OF THE B.P.A. asked me to step down as Hon Secretary so he could appoint K.R.C LETTS, an ex- military man as full-time secretary. K.R.C. Letts became full time secretary in 1966.

3rd DECEMBER 1961.

Air Navigation order exemption allowing B. Green, Mike Reilly and Stan Anstee to parachute into Blackbushe Airport. Signed by Group Capt. Caster.

BLACKBUSH

This turned out to be very interesting as on the day there was a weather front closing in. Blackbush was in a large circle of clouds. We took off in the centre of the weather front and jumped as the airport flag showed nil wind. We fell for thousands of feet down the side of the massive grey cloud which looked just like a solid cliff. For one crazy second I flinched as I thought I was going to hit it. Just after we landed the wind stopped became so fast it stopped the aircraft from flying. It was exciting and allowed me to understand the excitement for guys that jump off the mountain cliffs and fly 'The Wings'.

STAPLEFORD TAWNEY

1961. I opened Club at Stapleford Tawney with Pat Slattery as Chief Instructor.

BRITISH SKYDIVING LTD. THRUXTON

At the same time that I was the first Secretary of the BPA, I set up my next adventure, the first Skydiving School in the UK. This was called British Skydiving Ltd. and operated at Thruxton Airfield near Andover, Hampshire. Shown in the photo below.

THRUXTON AIRFIELD

In the above photo the runway that runs towards the top of the page is the longest runway. In the story 'Overloaded' had we been on any other runway I am sure all of us on board the Rapide would have been killed. That is when fate or tremendous luck steps in. The control tower at Thruxton Airfield is on the eastern side of the airfield.

THE CLUB PARACHUTE PACKING ROOM

It is not a good photo, but it is the only one I have. Penny Seager and Christine Pearson were here.

THE B17 FLYING FORTRESS

9th & 10th JANUARY 1962

ACCIDENTAL DEATH

I had been employed to organize the parachuting for a film, THE WAR LOVER. The lead actor was Steve McQueen. My part in this film, acting as the Co-pilot told to jump from the B17 and then pushed out the bomb-bay by the pilot, Steve McQueen. The timeline was the 2nd World war. This was over the English Channel and then to be picked up an M.T.B. That is a Motor Torpedo Boat.

Peter Lang was part of the crew along with Mike Reilly, Tony Miller and Dennis Smith.
I regret that I cannot remember the other two names, I think the chap on the left was in the SAS. We were using Seat Type Second World War 24ft diameter parachutes.

9th January.
Dennis Smith got concussion on the first jump. I bent my sternum by the large 'Quick Release Box' on the British seat type harness.
Tony Miller could not find his ripcord so used his reserve chute which we had fixed to the seat-type harness with two D shackles. He hurt his ankles landing on the tarmac runway. We all did three jumps in less than five hours from the B17 at 2,000ft onto Manston Airfield in Kent.

Next day, the 10th January 1962, the film director required me to exit through the bomb bay acting as the co-pilot that gets kicked out the plane by Steve McQueen who played the pilot. McQueen then attempts to save the doomed plane but crashes into the White cliffs of Dover.

This jump entailed landing in the cold water of the English Channel. 12miles off Newhaven.
My good friend Mike Reilly was with me just for the ride, all dressed up as we had already jumped over land three times at Manston Airfield in Kent,

pretending to be the crew evacuating the doomed plane. Mike and I had had dived out of the side gun turret and the other guys had dropped out of the open bomb doors. The film clip that was accepted shows me rolling along the fuselage because I did not take a running dive out of the side gun door. I was lucky to go under the tail-plane instead of wrapping my-self around it.

FOR THE TOSS OF A COIN

We were in the air on our way to the English Channel the pilot was John Crewdson. There was one engineer on board, Mike Reilly and I were in the bomb bay. At this moment Mike began to chat and said, "I've not had the chance to jump the bomb-bay, please let me do this jump I will forever be grateful if you do." I replied, "Mike it's my job, my risk, your jumps on the airfield are done." He then said, "Toss you for it," and produced a penny. *It did not occur to wonder why he had a penny in the pocket of the American uniform.* "OK," I said, he tossed that fateful coin, he said "Tails" and he won.

We changed parachutes for the part, I did it with a heavy heart. I had prepared a dummy, a figure with a 24ft chute. Then after circling over the MTB, I dropped the dummy. The motor torpedo boat got to it in less than a minute, such a relief, we laughed.

We circled again. John Crewdson was one of the best pilots you could meet. The line-up was perfect.

Now with cameras rolling, it was time for Mike to go. He was a superb athlete, gymnast, and he played Water Polo. I had tried to play Water polo with him and only lasted a few minutes before I was totally exhausted.

The approach was at 2,000ft, as the pilot throttled back Mike exited at 1,500 ft. With the main parachute open he drifted down to land in the cold water right in front of the boat. The crew had hold of the canopy in seconds.

Then the first calamity; the engines of the boat were stopped by the crew. Then another misfortune struck, a gust of wind blew up! I was watching from above and felt fear. As the wind caught the chute and pulled Mike away from the crew, burning their fingers on the nylon cords until they let go!

He was drowned by being dragged across the water. Being dragged like this caused the water to flow over his inflated lifejacket and his head. By the time the boat crew restarted the engines and caught him he had drowned.

At the inquest it was established that the crew

had stopped the engines to pick up Mike. After the wind dragged him away, they had to start a small engine called a donkey engine to restart the main engines which took too much time to save Mike. But for the toss of that penny, I would not be here, I think that Mike's death took a lot of my enthusiasm for the sport away.

UNDER THE WIRES

On an earlier filming flight, I asked the pilot John Crewdson if I could accompany him. I was totally unaware of what he was going to do. The scene required the B17 to crash into the White cliffs of Dover; In order to achieve this effect, the camera was placed in the tail and in the finished film runs backwards. Look for the seagulls flying backwards to check that out.

I laid in the Perspex nose cone, looking forward to the flight. After flying around looking for a suitable site, John flew inland and approached the coast. There were massive national grid power lines were running parallel to the sea on top of the cliffs. To my utter amazement he was flying across the Kent farmland aiming to fly under the wires. I tried to turn and scramble to a safer place than the nose cone but hit my head very hard on the fuselage. I decided I would be killed in the rear anyway, so I laid back down to watch. He flew under the wires then closed the throttles to the four engines, the plane sunk below the cliff, camera's filming.

In the film it will look as though the pilot is desperately trying to get over the cliffs. Then John slams on the throttles and climbs steadily across the sea. He then turned inland for another attempt. I had seen two ships approaching from the East and the West. We go under the wires again then down, skimming over the sea we pass between the two ships with plenty of room. But he goes around again for the third time almost cutting the grass; the ships are very close now. We go between them, two coastal cargo vessels, not the mountainous container ships of today. As we pass between them, I wave at the lookout's standing on the ship's bows, they can clearly see me as **I look up at them**! They return the wave.

As we landed from this last fateful flight at Manston Airfield the undercarriage collapsed. The port undercarriage came right up through the wing. Had it collapsed on the earlier flight the sea scene most probably would not have taken place. **That is fate.**

Note. Bear in mind this was a WW 2, B17 Flying Fortress that had stood mothballed in the Nevada Desert for over twenty years.

THE INDIAN ROPE TRICK

Ray Etchell and I were free-falling from 12,000 ft, at Thruxton Airfield, this was a high as the Rapide aircraft could climb with eight parachutist's and the pilot on board. This was just right because you require oxygen above this height. A lot of people do not realize that the commercial aircraft keep the passenger cabin pressurised to around the pressure of 6,000ft. Lack of oxygen is insidious in that you do not realize what is happening to you until it is too late and you become unconscious.

With the lowering of air pressure above 5,000ft the interior of the plane becomes quite obnoxious if the lads had too many beers the night before and especially if they had eaten baked beans. Despite having the door open, very often the pilots sprayed air freshener from the cockpit to kill the smell.

Ray Etchell was in the Parachute Regiment and as he was the same size and weight as my-self we jumped together a lot. We were always looking for something different to do, like jumping with small drogue chutes which gave a feeling like Mary Poppins hanging under an umbrella. One day we got a rope about 20ft long and jumped from 10,000ft holding each end. We were curious about the effect it would have.

As I left the plane first more or less pulling Ray out of the door, the visual effect was weird because it looked like Ray was balancing above me on a stiff rope. To Ray it looked as if I was hanging on the bottom with the earth below and if he let go, I would fall? We then came level with each other and knew that we were turning as we could see the scenery below rotating. Later we were told by ground observers that we were spinning at high speed like a helicopter blade.

I was really enjoying my-self when I felt a jolting on the rope. I looked at Ray, he was shaking and jerking me back to reality, he signalled that he was pulling his ripcord and looking down I realized we were dangerously close to the ground (1,000ft)
He was risking his life to ensure that I woke up out of my reverie.

What happened was the high rotation speed was spinning the blood out of my head towards my feet and I was losing consciousness without realizing it. Ray had previously told me he wanted to die when he was still relatively young and handsome. But he lost his young life in a car accident in which resulted in a fire, his feet were trapped, and he could not get out. He is buried in the Military Cemetery in Aldershot.

RAY ETCHELL OVER THRUXTON.

Ray was in the Parachute Regiment at Aldershot.

A fun guy, with a devilish humour.

RAY ETCHELL of the Parachute Regiment.

In this photo he was getting ready to
Jump for the film 'You Must Be Joking'.

Also, in this chilly adventure was John Meacock
and Mike West.

CHARLIE SHEA-SIMMONDS
OVER THRUXTON

We had a clubhouse but on a nice day we would pack on the grass. We had a big Bedford ambulance, but its main use was for transporting kit and students. The club quickly became very popular with hundreds of members. If you missed the airfield it did not matter, the countryside open and beautiful, the farmers friendly. Of course, the instruction was excellent as well. There were other factors at play.

During the 1960s we soon became operative full time. As there was no limit on the height at Thruxton and the huge airfield was surrounded by farmland it quickly became extremely popular. If you wanted to take part in the sport, having signed up; you could arrive on a weekend and the next day be suspended under a parachute. This having been opened by a static line attached to the aircraft.

After six or more static line jumps, if you proved able you would progress to free-fall and count five seconds before pulling your ripcord. You had a second parachute on the front of your chest should anything go wrong with the main chute. Students would progress in 5 seconds stages to develop the art of remaining in a stable free fall position preparatory to learning to turn, manoeuvre and execute aerobatic moves.

I had purchased American Air force parachutes; the Americans sold them after they had been in storage for ten years. They were brand new! I then modified them to have a forward speed and the ability to turn, better to see where you were going. It was very disconcerting to land flying backwards especially if trees and barbed wire is involved. Very soon we had ten instructors and a converted Tiger Moth aeroplane G-APAM.

This was converted to carry a pilot plus two parachutists. It had a strange title for this modification: it was called a Jackaroo. This plane had previously belonged to Sheila Scott OBE, a famous Aviator. She had named it MYTH 2.

We got so busy I purchased a DH Rapide Registration number G-AKNN so we could drop eight parachutists on one flight. On good days when the weather was perfect for parachuting these aeroplanes flew non-stop from daylight to dusk. The pilot was John Collins and the airfield CFI was John Heaton.

One day a young lady had walked into the club house. I say "walked" because she was a local farmer's daughter. I could tell that she was from a good family, classy even though her clothes were often scruffy. She said "yes" instead of "yeah" and looked you in the eyes when addressing you.
Her name was Helen Flambert.

Years later when we had a reunion, I found out that she had become a radiographer. I became so impressed with this young lady that I named my daughter after her. I will try and explain why I became so impressed, that's in the story called The Shuttlecock.

She was also featured in the Tatler & Bystander magazine of 5th August 1964 in an article called The Para Girls. There is a superb picture of Helen in free-fall looking up at the aircraft with the Thruxton runways below. There are also photographs of Penny Seager who represented Britain in the World Championships and an interesting photo of 17yr old Jackie McGovern who was the youngest-ever girl parachutist in the UK.

PARACHUTING (THE SUIT)

It was a beautiful sunny Sunday at Thruxton Aerodrome. The British Skydiving Club instructors were busy dropping student parachutists on static lines from the club Jackaroo aircraft G-APAM.
It was a Tiger Moth converted into a four-seater.

Peter Lang arrived at the club; he had been my instructor for my first jumps at Fairoaks aerodrome, Nr Woking sponsored by the GQ Parachute Company. Peter introduced me to his wife, they had just got married. He worked in the fashion industry for a company called 'Berketex' and was always immaculately dressed. This day he was wearing a beautifully tailored grey striped suit, white shirt and silk tie, I also noted the handmade shoes.

Peter asked me if he could despatch a student. 'despatch' did not mean causing the poor student physical harm but to travel in the aircraft and instruct the pupil when to jump. I agreed and he said he did not wish to jump after the student, but he borrowed a backpack parachute for safety reasons and donned it over his suit.

His pupil was to do a static line jump. His wife and I walked out to the drop zone in the middle of this huge grass airfield and arrived at the target area as the plane came overhead at 2,500 ft.

We could see the student climb out onto the starboard wing of the Jackaroo aircraft and then jump, rather quickly I thought. At the same time another chute opened on the port side. "Peter never said he was going to jump." I said to his wife as we watched the two descend.

Peter came floating down quite close to us. It was a good example of spotting. I say floating because he was of light build. When he descended close to us, we could see that he did not have a helmet or reserve chute. His suit was in torn and his face and shirt slightly bloodied. "What happened," we chorused as he landed. He was not seriously injured but had numerous scratches. He and the student then explained what happened.

Peter had directed the pilot to the exit point and asked for the engine speed to be reduced then he told the student to climb out onto the wing. The student had to wait for the instruction to jump. As the student looked at Peter, he saw Peter's parachute pack snag on the upper part of the open cockpit and pop the pack open.

He tried to tell Peter but could not because of the engine noise; he saw the parachute drifting out over the pilot's head into the slipstream. Peter was shouting for him to jump and was oblivious of the danger he was in. The student very wisely decided it was time to leave, at the same moment Peter's chute was streaming out into the slipstream over the tail-plane and then it opened pulling Peter out of the aircraft. But not out of the door but through the fuselage, ripping out the tough laminated wooden door frame that was at least 30mm square in thickness. He must have partially travelled over the pilot. Luckily the chute slid off the tail-plane, but the tail was damaged to the extent that the pilot could only make left turns, he landed awkwardly but safely. The pilot recovered after a cup of coffee, but the repairs took a week. Peter's wife probably did not want to see another parachute jump but later Peter joined our team to do the parachuting for the Steve McQueen film The War Lover where we lost our good friend Mike Reilly.

THE JACKAROO

That is not lightning on the left of the photo!
The photo shows a club instructor despatching a student, the student's parachute is attached to the aircraft. It would have been at this moment that Peter Lang's safety chute floated out the port side and dragged him out. The Jackaroo was the perfect aircraft for the student to exit and as the student stood on the wing enjoying the view he could hold on to the wood frame that curves over the cockpit. Sometimes I had a job uncurling their fingers.

A CHILL IN THE AIR

I was definitely a male chauvinist pig, but that is how I was brought up. For example, when I got engaged, my father said to me, "You know that a wife is a chattel". I asked, "What is a chattel?" "A piece of furniture" he advised. I purchased a house called 'Wilmslow' a few hundred yards from my place of work, which was my father's café and bakery in the village of Runfold in Surrey. The house was in a quiet road with fields opposite, there was a footpath and small trees on the verge. To describe my attitude, I did not ask Ann, my wife; if the house suited her. Nor would I discuss what vehicle to purchase. I chose where to go on holiday. I would not carry shopping, push the pram or hang out the laundry. I did not wear colours, only brown, blue or grey. I was a man. But I wore an orange jumpsuit.

One day I walked home for lunch, it was not ready, so I had to go back to work. I would not go hungry; after all I was working in a café. I had said to my wife, "I want my food ready on the table at lunchtime." Next day when I arrived, my lunch was on the table. It was spaghetti on toast; I was content until I found that it was stone cold. "What are you playing at?" I asked. "You said you wanted it on the table, there it is." Ann replied. "You are a housewife, what the hell have you been doing."

I asked, then without waiting for an answer, I looked around at her large collection of Cacti. I said, "Watering your plants I suppose." Then picking up the plate of cold spaghetti, threw it at the wall; where it stuck for a while, then slowly slid down leaving a pink trail. I picked up one of the plants and threw that at the wall. It exploded like a small hand grenade, showering black dirt like shrapnel.
I thought it looked spectacular, like indoor fireworks, so I threw a few more. Then feeling very pleased with my-self and very masculine, I went back to work.

All women reading this will now be shaking with rage at my behaviour.

At five pm, I walked around the corner towards my home. It was a lovely summer evening, a warm breeze blowing down the road. I was at peace with the world. Oh, it has been snowing; I thought. The hedges and small trees were covered in snow, the gardens were white. This cannot be? It is summer;

I was convinced it was snow right up to the very moment I touched it, on the tree outside my house. Sorry ladies, our house! It was a white parachute and all down the road in gardens and draped over the hedges were my parachutes. It is very strange that sometimes the brain will not accept the obvious.

Besides working in the café bakery, I was Secretary of the British Parachute Association and operating a Parachute club called British Skydiving Ltd.
I was also modifying government surplus parachutes for civilian use. I had stored them in the large front bedroom of our house.

My wife had opened the bedroom window, then held out each parachute into the wind, and pulled the ripcord. There were well over twenty parachutes down the road. This was a large amount of money draped over the hedges, and road. It found it strange that none of the house holders or anyone that passed by stopped, inquired what was happening or offered to help. As I entered the house, I saw that my darling wife had also emptied boxes of assorted brass grommets out of the window. This amounted to thousands of pieces which I used in the manufacture of cotton sleeves that were used to slow the opening of parachutes when skydiving. (That was done to stop bruising)

I walked into the house and said to Ann, "OK can we call it quits and will you help me collect all the parachutes. It is a lot of money to lose." She did, the main chutes had 28 lines and the reserves 24; it was a tedious job picking them carefully off the hawthorn hedges. But we did it before it got dark.

This incident started a new chapter in our relationship. We had three children over twelve years but ended up separating in the 1970's.

Both she and I remarried, but before I met my new partner, I knew that I had to change to become 'A New Man'. I am no longer the same person, I hang the washing, carry the shopping and I ask my wife what she thinks before any action or spending any money.
I am not silly. She does accounts.

GINGER GREEN

When there is an accident, there are usually several reasons as to why it occurred. One reason might turn out to be an incident that the participant can discuss later in the club or pub. But when other elements occur the combination can cause serious injury or be fatal. My first example is about "Ginger," Mr Green who was a friend of mine from Fleet in Hampshire. He started parachuting at the British Skydiving Club, at Thruxton in the early 1960s. He was a painter-decorator by trade and was fit, muscular and of medium build. He progressed to Free-fall and was a competent and safe skydiver.

He met a lady and then did not attend the club for a few months.

One day he arrived and introduced the lady that he had just married. He told me that he wished to demonstrate to her his prowess in the sport. I had no worries about his ability, it was a fine day with a light wind, and the students were already jumping from the club De-Havilland Rapide aircraft.

The airfield was a huge grass expanse with a tarmac runway and a tarmac track around the perimeter. Ginger's parachute was an American C9 28ft circular chute with a double L cut-out for turning and forward drive. There were no apparent problems. He drifted down and landed on the runway. But for some reason he broke his spine and was never able to walk again. I was very impressed by the loyalty and care that Gingers wife gave to him.

SUMMARY

When I was talking to Ginger later at Stoke Mandeville Spinal Hospital, he told me that during the week before the accident he had fallen off a ladder and injured one of his knees. He most probably would not have made this parachute jump under normal circumstances, but he wanted to demonstrate his prowess to his wife. As he came to land and unable to avoid the hard runway he thought about his injured knee and decided to land on one leg. This action caused his spine to twist and break on the impact.

Here we have five apparently unconnected reasons for this tragedy. First. There was the knee injury. Second. There was a gap in training and the instructors were unaware of the knee injury. Third. His desire to demonstrate his ability to his wife overcame caution. Fourth. His decision to favour one leg on landing. Fifth. Unfortunately landing on the hard-tarmac runway. He might have got away with it on the grass or the ploughed ground around the edge of the airfield.

THRUXTON. PACKING THE C9s.
The club ambulance is in the background.

COMPANY AMBULANCE

1962 The company purchased a Bedford Ambulance and a Peugeot Estate car, registration 5668 VB.

The ambulance's main use was ferrying students and the kit around the airfield. And attending shows.

THE ENIGMATIC SMILE

25th SEPT 1962

In the 1960's, the Military had not started sky-diving and we soon found ourselves inundated with soldiers of all ranks and regiments. Many were from the Parachute Regiment, Green jackets, Royal Marines and SAS. Obviously, the men from the Parachute Regiment progressed very quickly as they had done military training and static line jumps. Some names that come to mind are Cpls Vatsndal and McCardle of 1 Para. Don McNaughton of 2 Para. Sgt Mick Turner. Bob Ackerman of 63 Coy RASC. Ray Etchell of the Parachute Regt. Lt Shea-Simmonds of 3 Para and Lt Seager of the Royal marines.

The influx of members allowed me to purchase my first plane. It was a Tiger Moth converted to a four-seater and capable of carrying a pilot plus instructor and pupil or two competent skydivers to a height of eight thousand feet at a reasonable cost. This plane had been owned by Sheila Scott OBE of aviation fame and was named Myth11 with a registration of G-APAM.

It was a beautiful summer day and one of my pupils from the Parachute regiment was waiting to jump. He was a Corporal. I will call him Bob. He was keen and had purchased his own parachute. He was taller than me; close to six ft tall, he had broad shoulders, a typical Parachute Regiment man. He was looking very smart in his overalls; white helmet and expensive French Para-boots.

He had reached the point where he was doing a 10 second delay before opening his chute. I advised him that after the first chap had jumped from the aircraft to advise the pilot to do another circuit and he could direct the aircraft to the point where he would exit the aircraft. This point would be at the upwind side of the aerodrome and he would drift under his chute to the cross placed in the centre of the airfield.

As Bob stood beside the aircraft, the engine was ticking over. The other more experienced jumper who did not require any tuition started to climb on board. I instructed Bob on the procedure I wished him to follow. "Take your time on your circuit; exit the plane at 3,500ft, 10 seconds delay." He looked at me intently with his blue eyes. "Keep a basic free fall position", I instructed, this entailed holding arms and legs and akimbo like an X and facing the earth, "OK enjoy your-self."

By this time, he was climbing onto the wing. He looked down at me and smiled. As I stepped back out of the propeller slipstream, I thought to my-self "that was odd." His smile was not the usual fleeting smile which appears at the corner of a male's mouth and then disappears in seconds. It was a soft, lingering smile. But he was all man, a Para, tough and a square jaw that looked a bit Neanderthal. Now I think of it as a smile that says, 'I know something that you don't'.

I walked across the field towards his exit point. The club house was on the opposite side of the airfield. We had about six instructors busy teaching new students and repacking the chutes.

The plane would be busy going up and down all day as the sky was blue with small puffy cumulous and a perfect steady light breeze; a perfect day. The first guy dropped from the plane, executed his routine and drifted down on his red and white coloured chute. After his free fall of 10 seconds he would have a minute or more to enjoy looking at the undulating fields of Wiltshire.

The plane circled and came towards where I stood. The engine throttled back, and Bob appeared like a tiny bird; he immediately assumed the X position and fell for 10 seconds, then closed his legs with his arms outstretched looking like a "T" or perhaps it was intended to look like a cross. In that position he continued falling at 120mph. I was silently screaming "pull, pull, pull that bloody ripcord." After about 15 seconds he placed his arms across his chest. He was not making any attempt to pull the ripcord. I could see his hands quite clearly.

In the last few hundred feet, he rotated and hit the hard chalk ground on his back not far from where I stood. There was a tremendous sound "Boom" and he bounced approximately 20ft back into the air rotating until he landed again on his back. I ran over to him. His face was undamaged, and he looked like he was having a sleep except blood oozed out of his mouth, nose and ears. I stood looking at him, shocked and talking to him. "You stupid bastard why do that?" It was obvious to me it was suicide.

There were sounds coming from him like moans and groans. It was air escaping from his body. People started to arrive screaming "Help him, call a doctor, call an ambulance." "I said, No, call the police, he is dead!" Someone called me "A Cold Bastard", this was echoed.

The police and a doctor arrived, and he was pronounced dead. The club members went back to the hut and the parachuting activities continued, including those that called me names. It must have been tough for the new students, but it shows the mental strength that they had. I was asked to remove the parachute which I did. Don did not have any cuts or visible damage.

A young policeman then asked me to help lift him into the coffin. There was only the two of us. All the others had disappeared to the Control Tower. He got hold of his legs and I, his arms. I leaned back to lift and then stepped back. I looked at the policeman, he had a horrified look on his face. I thought he was going to be sick. I had not realized that almost every bone in his body broken, we could not lift him. We called for extra help; it took six of us to lift him gently into the coffin. Why did he do it?

That evening I called at his Barracks in Aldershot for I had his address on the records. I knocked on the door and a voice invited me in. There was a corporal sitting on a bed. He shared the billet with Bob. I had never met him before and as I entered the room and before I even spoke, he asked "Is he dead?"

"Yes" I replied. "Oh, I thought he would do it" he replied. "Why?" I asked. "His jaw, his chin, he thought it was too big, hard to get a girlfriend." I did not stay long, just left details. Nowadays men would have plastic surgery if they felt strongly about their appearance, but then I suppose it was in its infancy and expensive.

Then I understood the enigmatic smile, his secret thoughts as I instructed him. And his deliberate position of the "T" like the cross of the crucifixion and the final clasping of his hands across his chest. There was no last second change of mind. Bless him. Having recently looked at my records I know he opened his chute very low on a previous jump. I wish he had talked to me. If it was looks, the size of his jaw that he was concerned about, it is now quite common for men to have plastic surgery to change their looks.

CAMERA'S CAUSE CASUALTIES

Soon after I opened British Skydiving Ltd at Thruxton Airfield, Andover I had appointed John Clark as chief instructor. The BBC came to the club and asked for some footage of Skydiving activity. They fitted me with a camera on my helmet. All I had to do to operate it was to squeeze a button in my hand.

I asked John to be the subject; we exited the aircraft at 8,000ft and opened our chutes at 2,000ft. Everything had gone well up to this point. John was slightly above me and steered straight towards me, I could see him grinning at me through the camera eyepiece, but I had no concept of distance. Cameras also tend to make people lose awareness of immediate danger.

John flew right into my parachute canopy; he was actually inside the rigging just below the canopy. He was caught like a fly in a spider's web of 28 lines. In my terror I continued squeezing the button and filming as I watched him. What was liable to happen next, was the collapse of my canopy and I would be hanging below him, two people on one chute meant at least broken legs for me. If I jettisoned my chute and dropped away to use my reserve, my discarded chute would envelop John and result in certain death for him.

Then I saw John was carefully counting the lines and pulling himself towards his entry point hand over hand, there he pulled the cords apart and made his exit. This was a fine example of cool and calculated thinking, so years later I was not surprized to find out that he was a Barrister practising in Australia.

A belated thank you to John Clark.

DISPLAY TEAM

BRITISH SKYDIVING LTD DISPLAY TEAM

In the photo below the team are embarking on a hired De-Havilland Rapide to drop into a show. John Clark, Bernard Green, Pat Slattery and Doug Nokes. The person climbing into the aircraft is Desmond (Des) Smythe. I was told that Des joined the Australian Army and got killed in Vietnam.

YOU MUST BE JOKING

This is me dressed up to parachute into a Victorian garden near Elstree Aerodrome for the film 'You Must be Joking'. Below is Mike West, John Meacock and Ray Etchell. We had no idea that we would be wearing a kilt for the jump, and in icy weather. We were standing in for Lionel Jeffries, the star of the film who was supposed to be a Scottish Sergeant

Major flying back to London after a Treasure Hunt. When we turned up at Elstree aerodrome, and the film 'Wardrobe man' gave us the kilts we thought he was having laugh! After we accepted the idea of the kilts, we were handed large sacks and a 5ft sergeant majors baton. We asked what we were supposed to do with them? The answer was to jump holding them! We leapt out the aircraft with a large sack in the right hand and a large baton in the left hand, Then, very quickly put the sack between the legs, pull the ripcord and steer into a garden full of tents, swings, swing-boats etc. It was John Meacock that landed in the middle of it all, that was a 'wrap'.

THE JACKAROO

G-APAM started out as a Tiger Moth and was owned by Sheila Scott who was a famous pilot and author. The aircraft was converted at Thruxton into a four-seater. When Sheila purchased a faster aircraft, I purchased it as I realized it was perfect for dropping static line students at 2,500ft and quite reasonable in time and cost to reach 5,000ft.

I purchased the De-Havilland Rapide when we had hundreds of experienced members turning up on weekends with the desire to get to 12,000ft for a one minute skydive.

BRITISH SKYDIVING LTD

DE-HAVILLAND RAPIDE

Charlie Shea-Simmonds is by the aircraft door.

Developed in the 1930s. The first flight was 17th April 1934. They were used as a short haul airliner.
The number built was 727.
Construction was of plywood and fabric.

Two Gypsy Six engines that have six inline cylinders, of 200hp.
The length of the aircraft- 34ft-6in. Wingspan 48ft.
Max Speed 151mph.
Service ceiling 16,700ft. I think that would be with just the pilot on board,
Rate of climb 867ft/m.

THRUXTON, NIGHT JUMP

The Instructors all thought it would be interesting to jump at night. On a pitch dark and windless night after the pub and the control tower was closed and the control tower and clubhouse in complete darkness. I don't know where the moon was, Are you sitting comfortably? Then I will tell you a story.

Our favourite pilot wheeled out our de-Havilland Rapide. I first met John when he landed his own Rapide at Thruxton after flying from the Channel Islands. He called out from the cockpit "Can you let me out"? I asked him what the problem was. He said there was not a problem. "Just let me out." He had got into the cockpit on the Island and then had the aircraft filled with boxes of flowers. There was no way he could get out until someone removed the boxes. He also carried live lobsters which would die if he flew above 1,500 ft so he skimmed the sea and skirted the hills until he got to Thruxton.

Eight of us were jumping. There was not even a glimmer of a moon, perhaps he had the night off? We trusted John to get us over the airfield. We had two cars with their head lights on at the upwind side. I was the last one out and I could not see any of the others in free-fall, I was not carrying an altimeter and counted of the seconds to fall the required distance. I did notice the horizon was lighter and it appeared I was descending into what looked like a huge black bowl. When under the chute and descending into the blackness I heard Thud, "Ouch!" then another Thud, "OW!"

I counted the thuds, ouches and ow's until I knew it was my moment of truth, I tried to relax. Bang, I hit concrete and fell against something hard and metal? A car put its headlights on and swung its light's around, only then I saw that I was on the refuelling area by the clubhouse. The square thing was the pump and I was lucky as there were metal pipes sticking into the air to vent off fumes.

Had by bum landed on one of those pipes I would be fuming, or worse still I would know what it was like to be stuck on a stake, another few yards and I would have been on the clubhouse roof. This was my lucky day; I mean lucky night.

An excellent illustration of skydiving at Thruxton. The only person I can name has the white spotted helmet, Neville Hounsome.

THRUXTON, LONGLEAT LIONS
1964.

Will the Longleat lions eat humans? I am sure they will if you are chopped up and bleeding. This was on my mind one day in the 1960's. John our Rapide pilot offered to fly us for a jolly outing as it was too windy to parachute, or we were too windy to jump. "Let's go to Longleat, I know the people there," said a girlfriend of one of the blokes. We knew that we could not land there but would do a low pass then fly up the coast to a seaside town.

There were four paras and four girls in the plane plus the pilot, that was a full load, now keep this a secret but we did not have seats or seat belts. We sat on the floor as parachutist's normally do. Nor did we take our parachutes, I felt quite naked without it. It did not take long to travel across the wonderful open countryside of Wiltshire; I did not put the door on so I could hang out in the breeze and heat from the port side Gypsy Queen six-cylinder engine.

This plane G-AKNN that was constructed in 1936 had two engines, double set of wings and mostly built of wood with a main wing spar of pine. The fuselage was covered on a linen fabric and doped to tighten the fabric and make it waterproof. It was nicknamed the Brown Bomber because it was a painted a dirty brown colour and it was too expensive to change.

We swung into the valley where Longleat is situated, John eased off the throttles and we sank down into the valley. Slightly more throttle and in level flight and only about fifty feet above the ground we flew past the front of Longleat house. I was fascinated to see a row of statues on the roof, why spend a lot of money and stick them on a roof?

My attention was then drawn to the lions running around because a great winged noisy monster was bearing down on them. I heard John increase the engine rev's and looked out of the door to see why. The house is in a valley that has a horseshoe shape and we were heading for the closed end of the valley. there was a wooded hill in front of us. Then the port engine coughed and started to lose power.

I thought, 'We are going to die!' I thought about the impact into the trees, the chopping of flesh and then the lions would eat us. To my surprize John shut down the engine, I thought No, No, then he very gradually increased the power until the engine coughed again and he held it at half power. Those with their eyes open watched the trees brush the undercarriage as we flew over with the starboard engine screaming on full power. Later John told me that the magneto cover had split, and sparks flew all over the engine when on full power, at half power the sparking was contained. The reason we survived was that john had owned a Rapide for years and understood the aircraft intimately.

These planes were used by the Scottish Airlines and were not built to be aerobatic. One day I was sitting the airfield bar when there was no parachuting due to a low cloud base. A helicopter pilot walked in and said he had just seen a De Havilland Rapide do a Loop the Loop above the clouds. "Was it a dirty brown colour?" I asked. "Yes." That was John taking risks with his life and my plane. But I had to forgive him because he was the best pilot we had. Also, he had saved us from crashing twice once at Longleat House and an occasion when there were ten of us on the plane instead of eight.

HAIRY SCARY FOR BABY BERNIE

1965.
One day when the wind was too strong to parachute at Thruxton we were playing with a 28ft B4 with a double LL cut out at the back. We were being dragged over the airfield sitting on pram wheels. Parasailing had not been invented yet and standard military style parachutes just dragged along the ground. I tied a long rope to a Landrover and tried to lift off the ground, but I was too heavy. So, I tied my five-year old son Bernard into the harness with leather belts and rope then inflated the envelope and let go.
To my horror he went up thirty feet or more and stayed there until we reversed the Landrover at about twenty mph to bring him down. I have never spoken about it till now. Something he really enjoyed was being tied to the floor by the open door of the Rapide when we jumped out and the pilot dived the aircraft down to pick up the next lift of students.

1965. British Skydiving Rapide G-AKNN

OVERLOADED

On a beautiful sunny day at Thruxton I joined a group of excited experienced jumpers embarking into the De-Haviland Rapide to jump from 12,000ft or perhaps a few feet higher. The aircraft had taxied to the end of the longest runway for a quick turn-around after dropping six students. We had the full length of the tarmac runway, about a third of the way down John shouted, "How many on board"? "Oh, Bloody hell-10" someone answered.

Enormous luck played a part as the take-off was towards the East, had we been heading West we would have hit trees at Thruxton Village.

I was by the door, with the engines screaming as we came to the end of the runway. I could see a small patch of grass and then a wire fence. Then the wheels hit the small grass bank and we bounced up over the fence, we stayed airborne at about 10ft across the fields, John could not turn the aircraft at all at this low level, Once again luck stepped in as there was a shallow valley ahead between two hills, he flew on gaining gradually height in inches. I gave a wave to people as we passed just above the roof of their farmhouse. We had covered a distance of approximately eight miles and in sight of Amesbury before John could gently turn the aircraft back to Thruxton. It was about after twenty miles that a couple of guys volunteered to jump out at about 1,500 ft. the rest of us had the luxury of jumping out at a decent height,

Those early types of wood, wire and fabric could absorb a lot of damage. The CFI at that time named John Heaton spun a Tiger Moth into the ploughed field near the control tower from an altitude of 6,000ft. He climbed out of the wreckage with a small cut and bump on his forehead and walked into the bar saying, "God does not want me yet, give me a whisky."

PLYMOUTH AIR RALLY
DUNKESWELL

17th JUNE 1962

Mike Turner was a Sergeant in the Parachute Regiment. He was an extremely tough guy. I think some of his subordinates called him 'The Skull', for some reason? There was a parachute competition at Dunkeswell Aerodrome. Luckily, I have this photo of the event. A great number of my photos disappeared when I lent them to a national newspaper in connection with the Farnborough Air Show.

PLYMOUTH AIR RALLY, DUNKESWELL

Pat Slattery, Des O 'Conner, on the left, Mike Turner on my right, Peter Lang is second from right, Sherdy Vatsndal third from right.

Dunkeswell was a delightful place to parachute as the countryside was of undulating hills with clean rivers cascading down the valleys and sheep everywhere. In later years when I sold the Rapide to the Royal Marines it was the sheep that used it for mountaineering practise and totally ruined it.

I recall there was a lot of talent there, skilled skydivers that were developing the art of flying in the sky together. Sherdy Vatsndal who was in the Para's and became a helicopter pilot. I remember he had purchased the latest type of chute called a Para-Commander; it was multi coloured. There were quite a few officers and other ranks and when they were parachuting there was no pulling of rank. Perhaps it was too dangerous to do that because accidents can and do happen.

Peter Lang was there; he was my first instructor at Fairoaks Aerodrome. Also, Lt Shea-Simmonds, he was brilliant at air to air photography and later became a pilot and flew the aircraft at Netheravon in Wiltshire for the Army Parachute Association.

Sgt Mike Turner and I competed in the final jump-off; we left the plane together. There was a brisk wind blowing as I came in towards the target with Mick behind me. I was tempted to take a downwind landing but thought, 'I've got to go to work in the café on Monday morning', so I turned into wind and thereby slowed the landing speed, but I still came in backwards with a thump. Mike was screaming at me "OUT THE WAY, CHICKEN" as he thundered in full pelt downwind right on to the target. He got the big silver cup and I got the tiddly little one. He laughed at me for turning into wind and said I could have won if I had not done so.

The next morning, he dropped his trousers and showed me his multi-coloured legs, from his heels to his hips he was black, blue, and a greenish yellow. That was a lot of punishment for winning a silver looking cup. Twenty years or so later I was in my café when he came in to see me. He was walking with the aid of a stick and he told me that when he left the Army, he bought a farm but soon found he could not sit on a tractor because of his damaged hips.

I did not learn any lesson from Micks multi-coloured legs, in later years I suffered a fractured spine by taking a stupid chance trying to stop the Halfpenny Green from closure.

On a visit to Stoke Mandeville spinal hospital to visit 'Ginger Green' he was the parachutist that tried to land on one leg because he had earlier hurt his knee.

That snapped his spine. Out of sixteen other men in the ward, one had been run over by a military hovercraft, eleven had fallen off from ladders and one dived off Southend pier in the morning and then dived off in the afternoon, but the tide had gone out!

THE SHUTTLECOCK

12th AUGUST 1962.

Helen Flambert quickly progressed through her static line jumps and proceeded on to free-fall, getting up to or rather falling, for ten seconds after leaving the plane at 3000ft and opening her parachute at 2000ft.

It was in June 1964 I was offered an Aeroplane called a De-Havilland Rapide for £3,000. The cost of a reconditioned engine that was permitted to fly for 1000 hours was over £1000. This was a fantastic opportunity. This plane was built in the 1930s of wood and wire and a covering of doped linen. It was very successful as the first airliner to operate in Scotland. It had two wings. I know you will think every plane has two wings. But this had two sets of wings one above the other; it had two six-cylinder engines called Gypsy Queens. It could carry the pilot and eight parachutists to a height of 13,000 ft. which took one hour to achieve. This was fine because you require oxygen above this height.

I did not have enough money to secure this aircraft, but Helen lent me £100 to help me get together a deposit until I got the rest of the money together. Shortly after this; my display team were asked to perform at RAF Finningley on the 15/9/1962.

Helen asked if she could come along as a mascot. I replied, "Better still I will drop you out at 2000 feet as a drift marker, instead of a toilet roll, it's a large airfield so you will not get into trouble, then the team will go to 12,000 ft." She was delighted. The team was my-self, Ken Vos, John Balls (now Ball) and Helen Flambert. The insurance taken out with The British Aviation Insurance co to indemnify the Crown was £2.10.0.

We drove into RAF Finningley in our VW van. We were stopped at the Guard house. The Sergeant said he was expecting us, and we were to be billeted in the Sergeants Mess. On opening the side door of the van, he appeared to be totally shocked by the appearance of Helen. Of course, this was in the days when the Forces were manned by men, and he disappeared to consult his superiors. On his return Helen was marched off, destination unknown, perhaps to the deepest darkest dungeons.

After the night in the Sergeants Mess; *it was not messy at all*. For those of you that do not know, it is a peculiar military way of describing where the Sergeants eat, drink to excess and sleep it off.

In the morning we were taken to the Officers Mess to have breakfast. Fortunately, we were in our smart jump suits. Then Helen was escorted in, she had been given a room in the Officers' Quarters. She was wearing scruffy jeans with her knees showing, a huge man's knitted jumper with moth holes and ragged elbows. This was long before Pop Stars made it fashionable to be unkempt. This was so out of place with the Uniformed Officers and the impeccable military waiters with their white gloves; they were serving breakfast from silver dishes. But Helen had that aplomb, the mannerisms, and the cultivated tone of voice which meant the officers gave her an extraordinary amount of attention.

The Air-show, after the briefing, we took off. We needed an hour to get to height. The excitement was building, viewing the unfamiliar countryside, enjoying the new experience of performing for the RAF; looking down at the Helicopters that were already performing their gyrations. Time passes quickly in these situations. Suddenly I was woken from my dreaming by Helen, "Bernard have you forgotten me? You were going to drop me out at 2,000 ft. and it is now 6,000ft." "Oh Sugar," I said or words that to that effect and thought for a minute or two.

I could not drop her now with the helicopters flying below. I had played badminton and thought of the stability of the shuttlecock. Helen was taller than me. I asked Helen to stand up "You are going to jump with me from 12,000 ft. You will hold a stable position with arms and legs wide, lower legs bent backwards and forearms also bent back. I will hold onto your front harness and curl up into a ball. We will look and act like a shuttlecock, a human shuttlecock, never seen or done before." She agreed albeit with a look of anxiety. Remember the highest she had jumped was 3,000 ft.

We did not have long to wait. At slightly above 12,000ft the pilot throttled back to reduce the slipstream. I stepped out onto the wing. Helen came to the door. I grasped her harness and pulled her out into the chilly air. When you are in the aircraft with the door open; it is noisy; in the doorway and on the wing, it is deafening; the engine and the whirling propeller right behind you. For the first few seconds we tumbled, then calm, a wonderful silence after the noise of 12 cylinders roaring through un-silenced pipes. We were perfectly stable, lying on a bed of air.

I looked into her eyes. It was a picture of abject terror, eyes very wide, and her body stiff but under control by her iron will. Or was it frozen in terror? Very quickly she relaxed, and a smile spread across her face, I asked "Are you OK?" "Yes" she replied. "Soon I will let go of you" I told her. It takes one minute to fall 10,000 feet. I let go of her after 30 seconds and was horrified for a moment because we did not separate. Looking down between us, I realized that a vacuum was holding us together, I pushed her away, watched her for a while and seeing she was stable and obviously happy I turned over.

The Team landed in the middle of the airfield. I watched Helen land feet away from the VIP tent. By the time she rolled to a stop she was by their low white painted fence. She pulled off her harness and a large Brigadier covered in medals and red and gold braid grabbed her and pulled her over to join the large assembly of officers. We did not see her again until nightfall when we had to start for home.

British Skydiving Ltd were invited back to R. A. F. Finningley, Doncaster, Yorks. We provided a team of six skydivers at a display on the 17th September 1966. The British Aviation Insurance Company provided insurance cover for the sum of £3-0-0d

COMPANY FORMED

25th SEPTEMBER 1962

To operate the Skydiving Clubs and deal in American Military Parachute Equipment.
The first title was Parachute Equipment (Surplus) Ltd. This was changed to British Skydiving Ltd.

SHOW CARAVAN INTERIOR

THRUXTON. CLUB MEMBERS

In the photo below, John Meacock in the red jump suit is briefing the students. John was one of the first to use the rig with the reserve chute on his back. There are students with static line rigs and the experienced jumpers are standing back.

In the photo below is Charlie Shea-Simmonds demonstrating the relaxed style of skydiving at the British Skydiving Club, Thruxton.

This position works like a shuttlecock with the weight at the low level and the airflow dragging on the legs and arms. All it needs is a twist of the hands and the skydiver will rotate left or right. Charlie became a first-class air to air photographer.

Charlie Shea-Simmonds.

A 7TU AT THRUXTON. 1962

THRUXTON, THE WILD SIDE

In the dark after parachuting had ceased, the club members invariably went to the George public house in the village of Thruxton. This village was part of a farming community. The pub lies in a short valley on the east side of the airfield and in the 19th century was on the main highway. Now there is a fast road on the south side of the village. The pub walls were made of wattle which is a combination of mud and straw, dung and sticks. The roof was thatched with a large overhang to keep the rain off the walls. One stormy night a sheet of tin fell against the outside wall and directed the rain onto the wall, by the morning there was a huge hole right through to the interior. Now back to my story. Opposite the pub is a shallow river, the water is crystal clear. It is only about eight feet wide and there is no bank or fence, nice for a paddle.

Pat Slattery was one of our experienced Skydivers, he came from the East End of London which was renowned for being a tough area and home to the Rag trade, Not rags but the place where clothes were manufactured. Pat liked to be seen, as a hard man and I thought he acted like a cross between Humphrey Bogart and James Cagney. He smoked but never lit his own cigarettes as he always got his sidekick to light it for him. His attitude might be explained by the fact that he was a 'Pleater'. That meant he was employed to iron pleats into dresses and kilts.

He started doing something quite naughty. When it was dark and the boys were in the pub, he would sit in his employer's 7cwt white van at the end of the road with the engine running and the lights turned off. That does not sound very naughty does it? But when a car ventured down the road from the opposite end, he would drive towards it and then switch on his headlights. It was a game of chicken, and the unsuspecting car would end up in the river!

He would continue driving around the village and back to the clubhouse. The car occupants had a paddle and luckily nobody got hurt, except when another club member tried it and he had five angry young men to deal with. Bob Acraman saved his bacon by dashing out the pub and dealt with the four angry males.

BRITISH SKYDIVING 'JACKAROO'.

John Meacock and Bill Catt standing in front of the British Skydiving Ltd Jackaroo aircraft at Thruxton.

The 'Jackaroo' could climb very well up to 6,000ft with two parachutists on board.
John Meacock eventually operated his own very successful Parachute Centre.

They are wearing the American surplus kit that we were all using in the early 1960s. B4 Harness with a C/9 Red and White rip-stop nylon 28ft canopy. The reserve had a 24ft ripstop nylon canopy.

Note the Capewell release system that enabled the release of the canopy in high winds or if landing in water. The British parachutes did not have these. The altimeters mounted on the reserve packs were WW2 aircraft altimeters.

BPA MEMBERSHIP

1963.CompanyAccounts. These accounts show that all British Skydiving members were required to join the British Parachute Association. The fees were included in their membership and course fees and then forwarded to Stanley Anstee who kept the accounts for the BPA.

14th FEBRUARY 1964
On this day I changed my company name to British Skydiving Ltd.

THE BROWN BOMBER

This is a group of British Skydiving members at Thruxton. Looking at this photo I recall an incident when the locking pins on the port engine cowling were not fastened. At about 800ft altitude the huge cowling rose up vertically and only the pilot's expertise kept the aircraft from stalling, he landed safely.

ALLO-ALLO

STAPLEFORD TAWNEY

After Pat Slattery obtained his Parachute Instructors rating, I set up a Skydiving School at Stapleford Tawney Aerodrome which is on the East side of London. It is 4.5nm east of Romford, Essex.
There was great potential with the large population close by. I made an agreement with Pat for him to operate the club on weekends and eventually when the input was increased for him to run it full time. I supplied him with a brand new 15cwt Volkswagen van and twelve sets of parachutes with all the paperwork and advertising. It all started very well but then the income started to diminish.

One Saturday I telephoned the airfield control tower and asked, "Any parachuting today?" They replied that there had been lots of parachuting all day.
But that night Pat phoned a dismal report about no parachuting due to lack of aircraft and pilots etc.

On the Sunday evening I caught a train and arrived in Walthamstow as it got dark. Pat and his wife rented a flat above a car showroom; I knew he would return there with the equipment in the van.
I was standing in the shadows when a policeman found me. "Allo-Allo what are you up to?" he asked. I told him that I was going to reclaim the van and

showed him the key. When I mentioned Pat's name he smiled, then nodded his head and said, "I will keep cavy for you." I had only ever heard that at my school when it meant, I will be a look-out for you.

It was unusual that he did not ask for my identity. He walked back across the road and stood in a shop doorway. It was not long before Pat arrived and parked on the side of the road, he went up inside the flat and the lights went on. I walked over, got in the van and drove away with the policeman smiling and waving goodbye.

It was a two-hour drive and when I got home the phone was ringing. I picked it up and Pat said, "You bastard." I corrected him and told him that I had telephoned the Airfield Tower. I told him that he was not playing the game, so our deal was finished. He said "OK." and put the phone down. It was a couple of months later that he came into my father's café on the A31 trunk road. There was no animosity shown or felt.

As we had a meal together, he told me that he was now a long-distance lorry driver. He still had that sharp edge, a customer appeared to be listening to our conversation, it did not bother me, but Pat swung round to face him and said, "What are you up to Mush, mind your own bloody business." Describing someone as Mush was derogatory.

There is a strange but true twist to this story.
In 1974 on my 40th birthday I played with an Oujda board for the first and only time. There were no parachutists at our party, and nobody could have known of Pat. The message was written down by a woman that I had never met before or since and she said "It does not make any sense" then threw the writing pad across the table, there were no spaces, full stops or commas, it looked like this-
PATSLATTERYLIVESNOTLONG. It was quite clear to me that it stated Pat Slattery lives not long.

There was another message from my elder son's classmate that said he died in a car crash in Canada while on the school holidays. Later we found out that this was true.

While driving his lorry Pat had a traffic accident which resulted in surgery and a plate being inserted in his skull. Not many years had passed when I was told that Pat had skydived from high altitude one morning and then scuba-dived in the afternoon, this caused his death due to the 'Bends.' That is an extremely painful way to die. It seems to me that Pat was playing the part of James Bond on this occasion and not Bogart or Cagney.

He was a devil and an interesting character, in the early days of running British Skydiving at Thruxton my wife and I came home one late night from a weekend of activities at the club. On opening the front door, the creaking of the door echoed through an empty house, no furniture, no carpets or curtains. We thought burglars had taken everything. But it was all upstairs in our bedroom, packed floor to ceiling and I had to go to work in the bakery at 4.30 am the next day. This was Pat and other London members work as they passed my house on the way back to London from Thruxton.

Many of the club members had excess energy to burn off and this meant that there were many extra night-time activities. Drinking alcohol was not done to excess because the members wanted a clear head for parachuting. Racing cars around the Thruxton track and runways at night was great fun. Some people's activities were unusual like climbing over the roofs of the Andover Town hall during the night.

People that Skydive seem to crave excitement and new experiences. It is the adrenaline rush. Some of the members had a penchant for speed. I certainly did and still do. I tried sailing after skydiving but then took up Hot Air Ballooning, which I really enjoyed so I became a balloon pilot, and this gave me a lot of thrills, spills and injuries.

Parachutist's/Skydivers were a great bunch of interesting people. I had many fast rides on a Vincent motorbike with Nick Grieve, he had been a motorbike cop. I still have a 11,00cc Kawasaki motorbike but with a sidecar, I fell of my bikes a few times.

It is unfortunate that some of my friends died when quite young, two from parachuting but Ray Etchell a Parachute Regt man drove too fast in his Mini and hit a tree. Another member Derick Springate of the 1st Bn Parachute Regt that I had spoken to about going too fast on his motorbike went around a corner too fast and met a bulldozer.

LANGUAGE

Derek Springate was from Bramton Carlisle.

He said to me. "When I were in Arab Dessert
I painted my name on all t-toys"
"Whose toys? I asked. "No, animals, the t-toise,"
he replied, with his accent from the north

He put his name on all the tortoises, he found
I was his way to be remembered, this lovable tyke.
Sadly, he hit a bulldozer on his motorbike.

MILITARY MEN

These military men in the photo above are waiting to board the aircraft. They are standing beside their Army Jeep. As they are not on static-lines they can go up in two's in the Jackaroo or eight persons altogether in the Rapide It was in 1964 British Skydiving Ltd purchased the Jackaroo G-APAM which was a converted Tiger Moth, MYTH 11 previously owned by Sheila Scott Aviator and Author. It cost £725.0.0. and was ideal for dropping students or two skydivers up to 5000ft.
For a price comparison an E Type Jaguar cost £2,200 about this time. And my house 'Wilmslow' cost £2,300 in 1956.

COLONEL R.D. WILSON

1st JUNE 1964.
SPORT PARACHUTIST. MAGAZINE
Page 3
The Chairman is now Colonel R.D. Wilson.
Hon Secretary, Group Captain W.S. Caster.
Bernard Green on the committee (twelve members of the committee were military personnel).

Lt RUDGE PENLEY
KIDLINGTON

There was a young lieutenant from the 1st Parachute Regt who impressed me at the meetings of the BPA. This was when the British Parachute Association was in danger of being taken over by the military establishment. Rudge Penley was the only officer that impressed me with his impartiality when he stood up with objections at the BPA meetings to proposals that he considered unfair to the civilian members.

It was at Kidlington that he made fatal errors, the day was bright and there was little wind. He might have misjudged his exit point, but I think he was heading to land where we were packing the chutes near the wooden huts. He overshot and was now planning to land on the grass between the wooden ex-RAF huts. But he did not see the telephone wire between the huts. His feet caught the wire which tipped him over and he landed on his head. He died in hospital. I was devastated by the loss of this perfect gentleman.

I'll make a point here that if you are descending on a parachute and have missed the drop zone. It is very important to look for the poles and posts that carry the phone wire, fencing wire and electric wires. They can be seen when often the wires are not

THE DE-HAVILLAND RAPIDE

JUNE 1964 British Skydiving Ltd purchased the De Havilland Rapide G-AKNN at a cost of £1.000.00 followed by a reconditioned engine at £1.000.00
The engines only lasted for 1,000hrs
Note it took an average of 1hr to attain the height of 10,000ft, that equates to 100 flights to 10,000ft. with students being despatched at 2,500ft the turnaround was approx. 20minutes.

BRITISH SKYDIVING CLUB
14th AUGUST 1967

There were over 3,000 descents made at the British Skydiving Club at Thruxton in the five months up to 14th August 1967. It was the popularity of having our own De-Havilland Rapide aircraft which I purchased in June 1964 and having full time Parachute Instructors and a very good selection of American Parachutes with different modifications. The fact that there were no height restrictions and a vast amount of grass to land on that made Thruxton so popular.

According to BPA figures there were a total of 14,450 parachute descents made in England in 1966 nearly 3,000 of them at Thruxton.

I BLEW IT APART

In the photo below of a GQ parachute that I purchased in 1965 for £300. I particularly asked for gold and white panels, it is a good job I never asked for all gold.

The first jump I made happened to be from 3,000ft and the chute operated perfectly. This is when the photo was taken.

My next jump was from 6,000 ft so I had reached terminal velocity. After the canopy had opened, I was shocked to see all the gold panels torn apart.
It looked like a kitchen colander.

I thought that if it was a colander full of water, the water could not flow out too quickly and likewise the air would behave the same way. So, I rode it down and had a soft landing. The explanation given was that the gold dye had caused the nylon material to degrade and disintegrate when subjected to the high pressure when deploying at terminal velocity. That is why I said I was glad it was not all a gold colour.

This was the latest type of parachute conversion that was available. This photo was taken when descending on my first test jump from a 3,000ft 10second free-fall.

The cut at the back of the chute was called a 7TU. That was the maximum you could cut out of the chute without the danger of it collapsing.
Note that the front of the canopy is curling in.

Now you can imagine what was happening in the previous story 9TU-just for you.

GQ Parachute Company gave me another parachute canopy.

THE THRUXTON NEWSLETTER.

BRITISH SKYDIVING LTD.

14TH AUGUST 1967.

Toll House, Runfold, Farnham; Surrey
So far, this year has proved to be, full of records. We have achieved the distinction of being the only civilian club to operate its own De-Havilland Rapide. G-AKNN.
We were the first to own an aeroplane although not many of you will remember our Thruxton Jackaroo G-APAM. which although much maligned did a good' job in keeping parachuting going. It went to our club at Halfpenny Green, Bobbington, Stour bridge, Nr Birmingham in June 1965 with Mike West as Chief Instructor.

This year, to date over 3,000 descents have been made at Thruxton. 'It would appear that Jim Crocker has done a large proportion of them for in one weekend he made 22 descents. Last year according to B.P.A. figures the total number of descents in the UK was 14,450. There is still plenty of room for improvement and if we are to keep the Rapide costs-down the more the better. I suggest every member should work on publicity, tell your local paper what a brave chap you are, "Local Boy rises to Great Heights'", and plummets down again.

The Rapide has flown over 50 hours since May but we will need approx.200 hours, a year to keep it going properly. She costs approx., £1,800 a, year without flying and then costs £12 hour to fly on top.

In 1965 we flew 83 hours in Mr Dommetts Rapide and 78 hours in 1966. So, you can see it is a gamble.
Here is a very rough break-down of costs involved:

STANDING CHARGES:
Cost over 3 years, incl. H. P. Charges approx. £350
Insurance £180
Hangarage & incidentals £320
Annual certificate of Airworthiness £800
Maintenance checks £150
Total £1,800
Therefore, if we fly 150 hours the standing costs will be £12/-per hour.

RUNNING COSTS:
Engine time, 800-hour engines are approx. £1,000each fitted, therefore per hour £2. 10. O.
Petrol consumption, 22 gallons per hour at 6/2d. =£6.15.8.
One and half gallon's oil per hour at 12/-=   18/-.
Spares and contingencies, average. approx. £2.0. 0.
£12 3. 8.
Standing Charges at 150 hours use= £12.0.0 per hr.
Running costs =£12. 3. 8. hour
TOTAL COST PER HOUR with 150 hours £24. 3. 8.

Therefore, if we fly 150 hours this year without too many problems or bad debts we should cut even. It is up to you to stop any abuse or damage to the plane because you are paying for it in the long run.

COURSES. I wonder if people realize that they can join in on any of the midweek courses provided they have paid the club fee of £5 per year or £3 for half year or 5/- per day. Contact the office for further information.

SPECIAL COURSE. October 1st to the 15th inclusive
John Meacock and John Burgess are operating a two-week course for all members static line basic and advance skydiving for the above dates. All reservations to be booked at Runfold as soon as possible the number will be limited to 30 in all

BPA COUNCIL NOMINATIONS.

14TH AUGUST 1967.

The Thruxton club members nominated the following people for the BPA Council John Meacock, John Harrison, Nick Grieve, John Cole and John Beard.

A BROKEN BACK

In 1966. I agreed to jump at the Air Display at Halfpenny Green Aerodrome Nr Birmingham, Having been told that the club would be asked to leave if there were no parachutes in the sky at the airfield that day as there was a parachute shown on the posters advertising the air show.

I had stopped all other parachutist's jumping that day because of the high winds, I was advertising this relatively new British Skydiving club. I went up on a Tiger Moth to 4,000ft and as I stood on the wing, I realized that relative to the ground we were stationary! I figured the windspeed to be 45mph.

Being worried about the club's future I stupidly jumped. The chute appeared to open behind me instead of above, the wind was so strong. I was whisked out of the airfield. I headed to a large grass field, then at the last moment I saw a double stranded barbed wire fence. I had a choice, be sliced in half or lift my legs over the fence, I did the latter and landed on my back. I knew immediately that I had severe injuries and laid very still, I twiddled my toes and fingers. Good they were working, I decided lay still and wait for rescue.

A Landrover stopped the other side of a low hawthorn hedge, a large man appeared and said, "I am going to bash your bloody head in." From my prone position, I asked, "Why" "Because of the horses." he said, "But there aren't any in the field." I pleaded from my submissive position. He shouted, "I don't bloody care, normally there are," as he hurried down the road towards the gate. I thought he will kill me if he touches me and he sounds mentally deranged. I released my chute and stood up, then moved the opposite way. He returned thinking I could climb over the hedge. We went up and down the hedge a couple of times until the club members rescued me.

I did not want to go to hospital in Birmingham as this event caused me to hate everything about the area.

I decided to drive home, but my legs had stopped working. As I had a Peugeot estate car with a bench seat, I got my girlfriend to work the pedals while I steered all the way back to Farnham, a distance of 140miles. Bearing in mind she had never driven a car before it was quite interesting but as it was dark there were not too many cars on the road.

A day later I went to my Doctor with the help of a friend and told him, I have broken my back. He told me "Go away, nobody walks in here and says such a thing." (he was an ex-military doctor). As I turned away, he chopped my shoulders with the edge of his hands and closed the door. I nearly collapsed in his drive; Two days later I pleaded for an X-ray which he begrudgingly gave me. Three days later he came running into the café to inform me I had broken my spine in three places, at my neck, between the shoulders and at my waist.

My luck held, when I saw the specialist a couple of days later at Guildford hospital (she was an exchange Doctor from Sweden) she said. "Had I seen you earlier I would have put you in plaster from head to foot." She added, "Then you lose muscle and it's the muscles that hold you together not the spine." She asked if I would like to do an experiment and have no treatment at all, just some Physiotherapy at a later date, I agreed.

For about a year I could not place my right heel onto the ground and my head was stuck so I could not turn my head. An Osteopath pulled my head off and although it gave me a headache for three months it enabled me to regain flexibility, and to turn my head while driving. I still could not walk properly.

I did not wish to be written of like a boxing champion that carries on fighting and gets physically and mentally destroyed. Neither did I want skydiving to finish me off. For about one year I could not place my right heel onto the ground or sit down on my buttocks. In the cinema I had to sit sideways on the seat in its upright position, using my calf muscles as cushioning. After wearing out three pairs of shoes in which the right heel never touched the ground, I went to an osteopath who fixed me, I tell you that was more painful than breaking my back. I swore at him but later apologized when I found I could walk properly again.

MY LAST SKYDIVE

I talked to my friend Sherdy Vatsndal, and we went to Thruxton in the middle of the week and used a Percival Prentice aircraft that belonged to pilot friend of mine. It was an interesting aircraft because it was the first all metal plane to be built by Percival. 370 were built and used by the RAF from 1947 to 1953.

It could not get much above 6,000ft on a hot day because it was so heavy but there was an attraction, the low metal wing.

Sherdy loaned me his multi-coloured Para-Commander chute which would give me a slow decent and waited at the edge of the ploughed field by the control tower. I told him that was where I would land as it was softer than the airfield.

At the exit point I said cheerio to the pilot as he was going to fly off to Elstree. When outside on the wing he shouted make sure the door is closed, I did and he pushed a bolt home, locking me out. You might think, So what! But it felt like being locked out of your own front door. I worried for a few seconds then turned and started to run down the length of the wing but found I could walk quite slowly and easily to the tip of the wing.

A walk in the sky! I had thought that that the slipstream would push me off. As I looked over the end of the wing, I had a strange experience. It appeared that I was stepping off the edge of a cliff and my body stiffened as I tipped off the edge. I have never ever been able to stand on the edge of a cliff or bridge as I felt as if I was being pulled over the edge.

Diving over I soon felt at ease and enjoyed the free-fall only to suffer a lot of spinal pain with the opening shock. The landing in the ploughed field was no problem, I told Sherdy that it was my last jump, He did not believe me. But it was. Shown below!
Sherdy, who was a superbly fit athlete and really nice guy, died in his sleep only a few years later.

MY LAST SKYDIVE

BOB ACRAMEN

I have always likened people to animals mentally putting them into a category and treating them likewise. There are plenty of snakes and rats and boring sheep. Bob was in the big cat family, a Cheetah, very athletic and with a devilish sense of humour.

He was one of my favourite characters that I had met in the Parachuting-Skydiving fraternity. I first met him when he turned up for a course at the British Skydiving club. He was a corporal in the Parachute Regiment, and I was informed by others that he was an Army Cross country champion and expert on the trampoline. His trampoline skills soon became apparent in his fast assimilation of the art of Skydiving. He impressed me at a very early stage by passing me in free-fall standing upright to attention and saluting me as he went past.

To illustrate his humour, apparently on one of the Rapide flights he realized that the new students were lost in their own thoughts. He climbed outside and hanging on the roof pressed his face against the window. When the unlucky student came out of his reverie and decided to look at the view, he got a shock thinking he was looking at the devil. Well Bob did have a devilish humour. (*For Americans humor.*)

One day I noticed he had lost his stripes, so inquired as to why. His Sergeant Major was telling him off for some reason and was wagging his finger in his face. Bob bit the offending index finger! It was not long before he got his stripes back. One thing was certain if you picked a fight with this wildcat then you would get bitten.

One memorable moment was when I was checking all the Parachutist's kit when they were getting into the Rapide aircraft. Bob marched up, gave me an exaggerated salute and said, "Ready for inspection Sah". He was not wearing the club equipment! I asked him about it, and he said he had purchased it. It was an American B4 rig with a C9 canopy, of the type we were using. He was wearing overalls with the knees ripped out and hiking boots with metal lace up hooks.

I pointed out that it had been known for rigging lines to catch in those boot hooks and hold you dangling upside down. I then saw that someone had tampered with the harness he was wearing. The harness could under the opening shock slide through the buckles.

I told him a Frenchman had been killed a week earlier when the two halves of his harness had come apart. Bob went white and started to walk away, I said "Bob it is not good enough to be a good Skydiver, you must look good also!" The following week he turned up with all brand-new kit and asked to purchase a pair of French Paraboots that I was retailing. I fitted him out and he promised to pay later. Weeks went by and although he paid for his flights at the club, he did not pay me for the boots.

I was running two cafes at the time, The Milk Bar in the Borough of Farnham and a transport cafe called Alf's at Runfold on the A31. We used to get a lot of Para's in there as they marched back to Aldershot after parachuting into Hankley Common at Tilford Surrey. I decided to telephone Bob's Commanding Officer in Aldershot three miles away. I explained who I was and said something like this, "Look this chap in your Regiment owes me for a pair of parachuting boots. It's a bad show and not good for the Regiments name. "He just said "Leave it to me!"

I thought that he would speak to Bob and then take it out of his pay. In the afternoon I was working on the café counter, there were about fifty lorry driver customers in the cafe when I saw an army jeep swing into the car park with two Redcaps (Military Police) sitting in it with Bob squashed between them. They jumped out and marched him into the cafe much to the amusement of the customers. The Military police said nothing, but Bob said "You Bastard. "I replied "You owe me the money, don't you?"

He shrugged; paid and then with a smile was marched out to the jeep. Much to my surprise he never mentioned it again.
The café customers thought it was very amusing.

POEM FOR BOB

ROBERT ACRAMAN

Robert was an educated, gentle gentile child
Only his family thought he was quiet, mild
But others knew he was precocious, wild
Entered the Army Parachute Regiment
Really that's not what his parents meant
They wanted a civilian, he would not relent

Athletic, army trampoline champ, a trier
Corporal in rank, he wanted to get higher
Reacted to RSM's abuse, consequences dire
Actually lost his stripes to his superiors grief
Mangled RSM's finger with his set of teeth
And started Skydiving, much to his relief
Nigeria his home now, a General my belief.

Note. The part of the above poem about the RSM was when he was a corporal and the RSM wagged his finger at Bob's face while lecturing him on being untidy. Bob bit the top off the RSM's finger so he lost his stripes.

HALFPENNY GREEN CLOSED

26th NOVEMBER 1968.

Meeting of British Skydiving Ltd in relation to the Halfpenny Green Club operated by Mike West. The club was not able to be profitable partly due to not having enough members and the high maintenance costs of the Jackaroo aircraft.
All equipment was removed from Halfpenny Green and the club was closed. The Jackaroo Aircraft G-APAM was sold for £501.15p
The Exhibition Caravan was also sold.

CLOSURE OF BRITISH SKYDIVING LTD

It was months before I could walk properly again following my parachuting accident when I had fractured my spine in three places. This was followed by some very painful physiotherapy.

On a fine summer day, I turned up at Thruxton to see how things were going. There were nine parachuting instructors at the club now that were earning some money on a part time basis from teaching, hiring out the equipment, packing the chutes and getting free jumps when they followed out the students.

When I arrived, I saw the De-Havilland Rapide at the end of the runway, so I parked close by it and went to the open door. I could see that there were only seven parachutists on board, and it could carry eight. "Any room for me" I asked, "Sure jump in." was the reply. There was always a fast turnover of students as only about ten percent continued jumping after their initial one jump course. There were no club instructors on this flight as they were all qualified skydivers.

As the aircraft climbed above three thousand feet one of the men started collecting money. He came to me and said, "Half a Crown". I asked, "What is that for" and he replied. "There are eight of us, we give the pilot the £1 and he knocks off a quarter of the flying time, Good eh". I gave him the two shillings and sixpence.

I did not wish him to know that I was the owner of the plane, as I did not have a parachute! The pilot could not see me and did not know I was on board, that could have been interesting!

When the plane landed, I told the pilot he would not fly the plane again. I then got the Club Parachute Instructors together and told them I knew what was going on, that the pilot had been taking bribes to reduce their flight times and thereby reducing the cost of the flight to all of the high flying skydivers wanting to go to 10,000ft which took one hour of heavy flying time. It did not take place on the short flights when dropping the students on Static Lines from 2,500 ft.

I started to explain to the parachute instructors that the Rapide engines were only good for 1,000hrs flying time and then they had to be replaced. What was happening was extremely dangerous. I had previously printed the costs involved in the club newsletter on the 14th August1967.

I knew what I was talking about as I had been on the Rapide when a previous engine cut out, luckily we were passengers on a jolly, no heavy chutes and only a half tank of fuel otherwise we would have ended up with the lions. We were flying past Longleat House at the Safari Park and we were only at rooftop height, I was looking at the statues that are on the roof at that moment the port engine coughed and lost power. That engine had done about 855hrs.

The pilot at that time owned his own Rapide and being very knowledgeable carefully kept it going by reducing the revs. I looked out the door at the lions and then realised we were in a valley, we only just cleared the trees and limped back to Thruxton. That engine was at around 950 hrs and I replaced that engine at a cost of over £1,000 plus engineer's time.

173

With a full load of kitted parachutist's, it would have been a different matter. There have been several incidents world-wide since when parachutists have been killed when engines have failed on take-off.

I was explaining that due to this cheating taking place by the people wanting to jump from the higher levels. The engineers and I would think that our Rapide engines had 750 hrs use but actually they would be at or beyond 1,000 hours and in a critical state, a very dangerous state.

At around this point 'Jim' who was one of the most active skydiver instructors said to the group "Pubs open boys, let's go". This was said knowing that I do not drink alcohol and did not like going to the George pub in Thruxton village.

Considering the danger that I had outlined and that they had all seen the 'Thruxton Newsletter' which outlined all the costs of operating the Rapide. Plus, there was no indication of an apology or show of intent to change matters I decided that I could not operate the aircraft with such a disregard for safety.

They most probably felt that I was financially too committed and that I could not close the club. They were also taking advantage of my absence due to my spinal injuries. This made up my mind to close the operation immediately as I did not wish to be held responsible for nine deaths, I had already attended three inquests and did not wish to attend another.

Within a week the Rapide G-AKNN was sold to the Royal Marines for £900.00 and they kept it at Dunkeswell Aerodrome, but they did not place it in a hangar. I understand it was totally damaged by sheep climbing all over it and urinating and defecating inside it. Perhaps the light brown colour made them think it was a special toilet for them

1968. Sadly the Jackaroo Aircraft. G-APAM had also been sold due to the Halfpenny Green parachute club running at a loss. I went back to running my transport café business ALF'S CAFÉ on the A31road at Runfold Nr Farnham, Surrey.

I then became a Commercial Hot Air Balloon Pilot which was a tremendous amount of fun and excitement. There were many strange situations and accidents which gave me plenty to write about.

BOB ACRAMEN, THE BUYER

Bob was now a Skydiving Instructor. I was in my cafe with a queue of about ten drivers that were buying breakfast at about £2.50 a time. Bob appeared at the back of the queue and shouted. "Do you want to sell your parachutes and kit to me?" I replied "Yes, it is all in my house down the road, my wife Ann will show it to you." He came back a short time later and agreed to pay £3,000.00 much to the curious looks of my customers. Bear in mind that my house cost me £2,200.00 in 1960.

I did wonder how he raised the money, but he did, and he bought himself out of the Army at the same time to set up his own Skydiving school at Thruxton and he made a great success of it. But eventually the airfield owner stopped the parachuting to develop motor racing.

When I next saw Bob, he told me he was a General in the Nigerian Army, teaching parachuting and Air cargo despatching techniques. Later I heard he owned a Nightclub out there. As I said, he is a fighter; a big cat! a cheetah, tough and fast.

TIM BETTIN, THE SKYDIVER

Free-fall did not take his life
it was everything to him
He was wed to it, like a wife
In heavenly blue skies
he flew for precious seconds
Only falling, say earthbound guys
When Skydiving, time stands still
space and air, a gymnast's delight
To use the parachute needs iron will
Never angry, I've never met anyone
like Tim, disk jockey, sold fireworks
an adult child having lots of fun

Dived into the depths of the sea
always looking at life's creations
with such passion and childlike glee.
We bounced Balloons off each other
sliding over and through the clouds
Skydived through them, with no bother
He joined an Army Display team
a severe oscillation while on the chute
The acute angle ended his dream.
His wit, delivered with a cheeky smile
and thoughtful sparkling big brown eyes
will stay in my thoughts for quite a while.

The above picture is the 1960s advertising poster for my clubs. In the bottom right hand corner was the office address. It is now a private residence. There were two versions of this poster. This one and another for Halfpenny-Green, Aerodrome, Near Stourbridge, West Midlands.

BPA 1960 TIMELINE
BRITISH PARACHUTE ASSOCIATION

23/NOV/ 1960 Letter from Sqn Leader Marks R.A. F.
HEADQUARTERS TRANSPORT COMMAND
ROYAL AIR FORCE. UPAVON. PEWSEY, WILTSHIRE.
Ref TC/48230/1/CA SQN LDR MARKS originally wrote to the Royal Aero Club but was informed by a Mrs Tomlinson to write to B. Green at Wilmslow. Runfold.
On the 29/Nov/1960 I wrote to Mrs Tomlinson of the Royal Aero Club, asking her to invite Sqn, Leader Marks to the next British Parachute Committee Meeting. He did attend on the 15/ DEC/1960
MRS TOMLINSON was Secretary to the AVIATION SECRETARY.

S24/APR/1961 LETTER FROM E.A.J. GARDENER ESQ, OFFICERS MESS 3RD BATTALION THE PARACHUTE REGIMENT, GUILLEMONT BARRACKS, COVE. It is addressed to, the Secretary, British Parachute association, Park Lane London. W1.

27/APRIL/ 1961 letter from CPL MICK REEVES Para Regt to B. Green Secretary of BPA.
Also enclosed my letter to Stanley Anstee Treasurer for the BPA. Enclosing the BPA memberships fees taken from four members. These four all joined British Skydiving for training in skydiving.

1/MAY/1961. My Letter to Stan Anstee, where I enclose BPA membership fees for. Peter Hearn. John Thirtle, Alf Card, S. Phipps. D. Francombe. *Why would I send this money to Stan Anstee if he was not the treasurer?*

MAY/1961 Letter from Cpl Mike Reeves SP Coy 1st Bat THE PARACHUTE REGT BFPO 606. Thanking me for information on the BPA and that he will attend the Para Championships on the 4th May.

6-7th/ MAY/ 1961 PROGRAMME.
BRITISH OPEN PARACHUTE CHAMPIONSHIPS
At Stapleford Tawney in Essex.
The wind speed was 20/25 kts. I did two jumps, 3000ft and 5000ft. It was continued at Kidlington Oxford 13/14th May. A Tripacer was the aircraft used.

Note. The programme stated, JOIN A CLUB For details write to B. Green, Esq, Hon Sec., British Parachute Association, "Wilmslow" Runfold, Farnham,
Surrey.

21/ AUG /1961 Letter addressed to The Secretary, Panel of Parachuting, Royal Aero Club, 19, Park Lane London, W1. This letter was sent to me by the Royal Aero Club. I replied to Mr Evans as Sec.

30/Aug/1961. Letter from RAF. COTTESMORE, OAKHAM, RUTLAND. Ref, Battle of Britain Show
Note cost, Insurance 15 shillings, Petrol 280 miles £2.10.0

30/AUG/1061 Letter from Research Bureau, Wells Organizations, 2036 Berkeley Square London W1
Addressed to, B, Green Esq. Secretary, British Parachute Association, Wilmslow, Runfold, Nr Farnham, Surrey.

5/ SEPT/1961. Letter from IRISH PARACHUTE CLUB. This was in relation to providing a Skydiving display at WESTON AERODROME Leixlip, Co, Kildare, Ireland. 17/Sept/1961. This prompted a story called THE BLACK HOLE

7/SEPT/1961 Letter from. THE BRITISH BROADCASTING CORPORATION. Addressed to "Wilmslow"

7/SEPT/1961 Letter from The Commanding Officer No1 Squadron 14th SIGNAL REGIMENT. Robinswood Barracks Gloucester. Addressed to Sec of the British Parachuting Assoc,

8/SEPT/ 1961 Letter from THE DAILY TELGRAPH, Addressed to B. Green, Hon. Secretary- B.P.A.

10/SEPT/1961 Letter from THE ROYAL AERO CLUB (Via Peter Lang) Replied as Secretary to BPA.

11/Sept/1961 Letter to Bernard Green, Hon Secretary, British Parachute Association, Wilmslow, Runfold, Farnham, Surrey. From, Squadron Leader Lockwood, R.A.F. Liaison Officer, Royal Air Force, WETHERSFIELD, Nr Braintree, Essex.

12/SEPT/ 1961 letter from Sgt Brady 144 Indep. Para Brigade, R.E.M.E. T.A. TA Centre Greens Rd, Keresley, Coventry. Replied as Sec to BPA.

13/SEPT/1961 Letter from HANDLEY PAGE Ltd
The Aerodrome, Woodley, Reading. Berks.

14/SEPT/1961 Letter from Major I.R. Critchley, BW, Brigade Major, 152 9H0 INF BDE (TA) Cameron Barracks Inverness,

15/SEPT/1961 Letter from THE DAILY TELEGRAPH addressed to   B. Green, ESQ, Secretary, BRITISH PARACHUTE ASSOCIATION. *This was in regard to Photographs I supplied to the newspaper for the FARNBOROUGH AIR SHOW which all disappeared.*

18/SEPT/1961 letter to Lt G.M. DAINTRY 1st Bn IRISH GUARDS, Caterham Barracks Woking Surrey. Addresses me in letter as Secretary of the B.P.A.
I advised him to contact Jim Basnett at Fairoaks.

21/SEPT/1961 Letter from T. LOCKWOOD Squadron Leader, R.A.F. LIASON OFFICE ROYAL AIR FORCE WETHERSFIELD NR Braintree, Essex. Addressed to Mr B. Green Hon Secretary.

4/OCT/1961 letter to Mr Acheson as Sec to BPA explaining About Clubs and costs. And that subscriptions to the BPA should be sent to Stanley Anstee, 37, Lambourne House, Silwood Estate, London, S.E. 16.

28/SEPT/161 Letter sent as Sec to BPA, to D. Corney explaining that his BPA membership fee of 10/6 should be sent to Mr Anstee 37 Lambourne House etc. And his nearest club was Oxford Parachute Club

4/OCT/1961 Letter to Wren Codd 118408 Rodney Division, Burgfield, Nr Reading Berks. Replied as Sec to BPA, enclosing list of clubs.

5/OCT/1961 letter addressed to B. Green Hon Secretary the British Parachute association. "Wilmslow" Runfold, Nr Farnham surrey. from Lt Harry M. Edwards USAF personnel services officer 20th Air base squadron, united states air force APO 120, US forces, requesting information on parachute clubs.

13/OCT/1961 Letter from the safety equipment officer WESTLAND AIRCRAFT Yeovil England. Replied advising him to contact Brian Porter of Graham St Swindon. Wilts as he operates at Staverton Airport.

1/NOV/1961 A Letter passed to me from Mike Reilly from a Mr Bautenback of Coventry, He had been advised by Flight Sergeant A.W CARD late of Abingdon to contact Mike Reilly. I advised him on clubs

29/JUNE/ 1964 DAILY SKETCH. Article with pictures of Jackie McGovern, Aged 17 yrs. Youngest Parachutist.
Her uncle was Malcolm Critchell was an experienced Skydiver.

5/AUG/1964 TATLER MAGAZINE Page 251 Jackie McGovern aged 17 yrs. parachuting at British Skydiving at Thruxton.

5/AUG/1964 TATLER. Page 252/253 Helen Flambert, exiting over Thruxton. Ref the Shuttlecock Story.

APRIL/1965. Set up British Skydiving Ltd club at Halfpenny Green, Bobbington, Nr Birmingham. With Mike West as Chief Instructor. Club house, a new VW Van, all parachuting equipment and the Jackaroo aircraft G-APAM.

25/JULY /1965. Article, full central page in the SUNDAY MERCURY. Showing Mike West, Christine Pearson and Carl Frith at the British Skydiving Club, Halfpenny Green.

SPORT PARACHUTIST MAGAZINE
1965

BRITISH PARACHUTE ASSOCIATION
BPA Magazine Vol No1. Page 16, THE THRUXTON LETTER, Photo of B. Green exiting a Tiger Moth this was taken years earlier at Sandown Isle of Wight at 6,000ft when I was using the GQ parachute No 352206.

Page 31 Advert for British Skydiving Ltd Office Toll House Runfold Nr Farnham Sy. And London office at Skyway House 125 Grosvenor High Rd London SE10.
Also, an advert for Paraboots at British Skydiving Ltd.

Note. The order form for the Sport Parachutist was to The Secretary General. B.P.A. &c Lower Belgrave St, London S.W,1.

BPA INSTRUCTORS CONVENTION.
3/DEC/1966.

31/DEC/1966 BPA ANNUAL RETURNS

NOMINATIONS FOR THE BPA COUNCIL.

J. Meacock. J. Harrison. G. (Nick) Grieve.
J. Crocker. J. Cole. J. Beard. N. Hounsome.
Note. All were from British Skydiving Club.

LIST OF B.P.A. PARACHUTING EXAMINERS

(Undated)
M.B. REILLY
J.T. BASNETT
Miss S. (Sue) BURGESS
A.W. CARD
N. HOFFMAN
P. LANG

J. McLOUGHLIN
M. MORRIS
A. CHARLTON
P. DENLEY
K. TEESDALE
A. MILLER

1967 SHELL AVIATION NEWS (MAGAZINE) Pages 12 to 16. Article on Skydiving at British Skydiving Club at Thruxton written by John Meacock.
Ex RAF Pilot Hugh Scanlon was editor of the magazine. Hugh was piloting the Rapide G-AKNN at Thruxton.

1967 BRITISH SKYDIVING Ltd. Company Accounts
Aircraft running expenses £1,348.15.4. De-Havilland Rapide G-AKNN. Original cost of aircraft was £1,000.0.0. plus, reconditioned engine after 250 hrs. A recon engine was good for 1000 hrs and cost approx. £1,200 fitted.
1967 G-AKNN insurance 18/3/67 was £66-0-0
Insured value £1,500 Third party £25,00.

1968 SOLD British Skydiving Ltd exhibition caravan.
1968 Closure of Halfpenny Green Club.

MY LOG BOOKS

I did not record many of my descents as I felt that as I has reached the top of my profession (as I regarded it) there was no one that could or would check my logbook. I stopped recording my jumps unless there was a particular reason to do so.

Some of the exhibitions were a totally different matter, when I was traumatized, I never wrote anything at the time but never forgot.
But the really interesting and exciting stuff like the Shuttlecock or the French Eagle then I did.

To explain this to a young person, I say that
in an experience like a car crash. You will remember every fraction of a second. And years later you will be able to recall the place, the type of vehicle, the colour, the participants, even their clothes.

ADRENALINE AND SANITY

To some people jumping out of aircraft and falling free before operating the parachute seems totally insane, but I found that Freefalling or Skydiving was extremely enjoyable. Before the jump and in the aircraft, you consider and reconsider everything that you have prepared. On one occasion I landed in the

aircraft in order to repack my chute because I had packed it in a hurry.
After having left the aircraft I would be perfectly relaxed enjoying the feeling of laying on a soft bed of air and being able to twist roll, spin and turn without the worry of landing on a trampoline badly or belly-flopping on water if the dive went wrong. Falling down the shear side of an immense cloud at the edge of a weather front was a thrill I will never forget,
It looked solid as rock.

At the age of twenty-eight I had never doubted my sanity, other people's yes, quite often. You might find that statement odd when I tell you that I have been a Parachutist Stunt-man Skydiver, and Commercial Hot Air Balloon Pilot.

I had read all the exploits of the early pioneers and deaths. Also, I had read all the Caterpillar books on numerous pilots that had bailed out of their crippled aircraft in the war. If your planes on fire you would not hesitate to jump but to jump out of a perfectly good aircraft. To parachute, you must have a deep desire to do it. To do the second jump is even harder. Your brain keeps saying, 'you have done it, why risk it again?' Only one person out of a thousand people will continue into this sport after having had the first jump. They are a particular type of person; I will not say odd because I was one.

I will make a note here about the type of men I was teaching. When I started operating my Sky-diving School many SAS, and Parachute Regt started their training with me. It had been the practice to use only officers to train as Army helicopter pilots. Then I was approached by the military authorities and advised that they wished to make an experiment. They asked me to recommend five army members of my club. All of them were corporals of various regiments and they all passed out as Helicopter pilots and instantly became officers. That was a great success story.

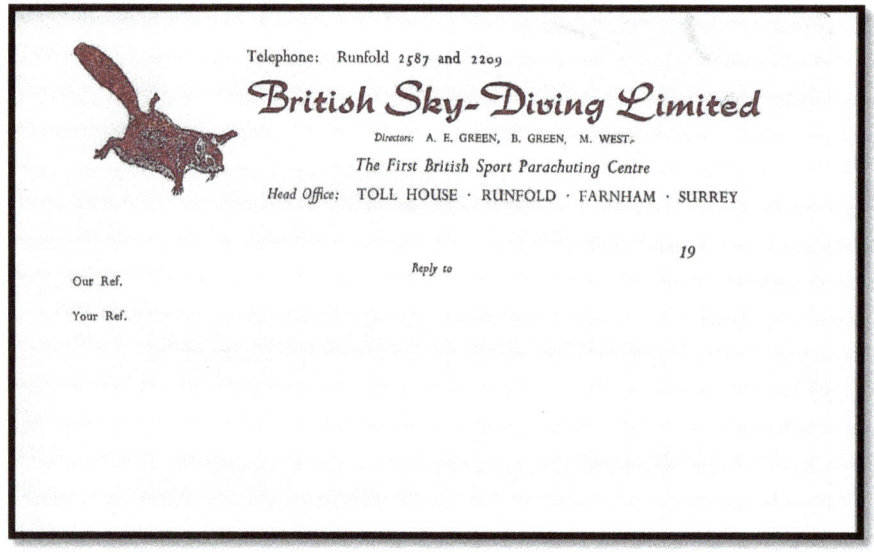

HEADED NOTEPAPER 14th February 1964

MY WIFE AND I AT THE BPA OFFICES 2017.
British Parachute Association Ltd
5 Wharf Way, Glen Parva, Leicester,
UK, LE2 9TF

FEAR

I want to tell you something that I find strange.
I have been almost without fear when leaping from aircraft. I say almost because any sensible person will assess the risks and think carefully about the precautions that he or she has taken.

I went to Wales once to try mountaineering with an expert. And although I trusted the ropes and the technique shown to me. I was terrified. I tried walking high paths in Switzerland with my son and daughter. As the paths narrowed so my fears increased. As we crossed a wooden bridge over a chasm, my son then aged fifteen realized I was nervous and started jumping up and down. I was screaming for him to stop while he thought it was so funny.

I went to the Lauterbrunnen valley in Switzerland this year (2019) with my wife and I thought that the above photo would amuse the reader when I explain my pose. I am hanging on to the metal fence as my legs were like jelly, I felt that I would fall over if I let go! It was all to do with the height and the sheer drop behind me. Any time I looked over a sheer drop I feel the urge to go towards it. I find it strange.

I have enjoyed remembering most of these stories, I do hope you will also have had a smile or two.

2015. I JUST HAD TO GET THAT FEELING AGAIN.

My wife Peggy (in black) kept trying to catch me but the glass was in the way. If you are thinking about doing Skydiving, I strongly advise that you try this first two or three times. It did not exist when I and my friends started, if it had it would have saved a lot of trouble and pain.

I have just been advised that Nick Grieve passed away on the 18th November 2019. When he joined the club at Thruxton he was 16 stone of muscle, he was a policeman with an innate sense of fun. Because he was so heavy I assembled a special parachute for him, it was a 32ft ex-military British Cargo Chute with an American harness and reserve. He never had a problem and never used his reserve chute.

In his later years he had a debilitating illness and I commend his wife, Maureen who stood beside him all the way.

Peter Lang also 'One of the Gang' also passed away this year.

BOOKS BY THE SAME AUTHOR.

MY WIFE & CANCER.
By B. A. N. Green.
ISBN: 978-0-9576042-5-4

A story of the mental trauma and difficulties met by the patient that has been diagnosed with cancer and mainly about the stress imposed on their partners.

DUNCE OR DYSLEXIC.
By Simpleton.
ISBN: 978-0-9576042-0-9

Bernard Green describes the difficulties he encountered in his early life, particularly his harsh treatment at school during the 1940s when Dyslexia was not a recognized condition. A poetic autobiographical wonder, this superb collection is interspersed with the richest of verses, speaking of romance and love, of odes to his clever loving wife as well as outspoken rhymes in defence of the environment and varied other conditions in the world that needs the voice of an advocate. Fiction is no rival to these true-life stories, a treat for the reader who loves adventures. Aesthete2000' allpoetry.com
Some stories are for adult reading only.

BUILDING THE KHUFU PYRAMID-SHEDDING NEW LIGHT.
By B. A. N. Green.
ISBN: 978-0-9576042-0-9

The author built a small pyramid to prove the concept to Professor Menno P. Gerkema of the Department of Chronobiology and the Department of Science and Society, University of Groningen, the Netherlands.

PARACHUTES, POEMS AND POLEMICS.
By B. A. N. Green. Autobiographical.
ISBN: 978-0-9576042-1-6

Bernard was a founder member of the British Parachute Association and started the very first skydiving school called British Skydiving Ltd at Thruxton, Andover, Hants.
Some stories and poetry are only suitable for adults.

RURAL LIFE IN RUNFOLD DURING WORLD WAR TWO. (Historical.)
By B. A. N. Green.
ISBN: 978-0-9576042-6-1

Bernard's life as a child. His father was dealing in the Black Market and taking his son, aged 10yrs with him on these ventures.

SPIES IN VUNG TAU 1915-1920
PHOTOS OF VIETNAM
By Bernard. A. N. Green.
ISBN 978-0-9576042-9-2

In 1987 the author purchased a box of early glass slides. There was no explanation as to their origin or content. He found that they were over one hundred years old. At first, he thought the photographs were taken in South America as they showed natives in forests with bare feet and ancient crossbows. After having the photographs processed into digital format, he realized that they related to a military mission by five men connected to Australia and Great Britain in the period of the 1st World War. This secretive journey took them through-out South-East Asia and Vietnam with visits to the Cocos-Keeling Islands. They spent a long time in Vietnam taking photographs which tell a story of why the French Military were building huge ex-naval gun emplacements at Cape Saint Jacques (now called Vung Tau). Narrative. Historical, period 1915-1920.

Available from IngramSpark.com as an eBook & Print on demand.

ZEPPELIN L15 & The Wakefield Gold Medal
By Bernard. A. N. Green.
ISBN 978-0-9576042-2-3

These are true stories about the Zeppelin airships that were built to wage war. So feared were these machines that they became known as 'the Baby Killers'. Sir Charles Wakefield, the Lord Mayor of London was determined to reward the first individual to shoot down a Zeppelin on British soil with a substantial prize.

How he eventually discharged this debt of honour, despite opposition from the War Office and exacerbated by class discrimination, forms a fascinating background to the story of the L15 Zeppelin and the Wakefield Gold Medal.
Sir Charles Wakefield eventually awarded 353 medals each weighing 1oz of 9 Carat (.375 gold) content.
But he was not allowed to call them medals and there was no official record kept. It took the author four years to assemble the names of 244 recipients. It is most probable that many of these medals have been melted down for their gold value.

berniegreen@live.co.uk